29/10/99 Rob. Garde 2/6×38

Managing the Secondary School

D1079352

This new edition of *Managing the Secondary School* brings up to date the consideration of the tasks and skills of the headteacher which was a feature of the first edition.

The book deals with all aspects of the headteacher's role including marketing the school and managing the budget. It also deals in some detail with the problems of managing change and with the role of governors and parents in today's schools. Throughout the book, Joan Dean considers the implications of the Education Reform Act and the National Curriculum.

Managing the Secondary School is essential reading for practising and aspiring headteachers of secondary schools. It will also appeal to school governors, to advisers, inspectors and consultants working with secondary schools and to those concerned with the appraisal and training of headteachers.

Joan Dean pioneered the training of secondary school headteachers in Surrey, where she was Chief Inspector until her retirement in 1989. She is the author of several books on educational matters, including *Special Needs in the Secondary School* and *Inspecting and Advising*, both published by Routledge.

Educational Management Series

Series editor: Cyril Poster

Managing the Secondary School
Second edition

Joan Dean

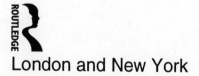

London and New York

First published 1993
by Routledge
11 New Fetter Lane, London EC4P 4EE

Simultaneously published in the USA and Canada
by Routledge
29 West 35th Street, New York, NY 10001

© 1993 Joan Dean

Typeset in Baskerville by LaserScript, Mitcham, Surrey
Printed and bound in Great Britain by
TJ Press (Padstow) Ltd, Padstow, Cornwall

All rights reserved. No part of this book may be reprinted or
reproduced or utilized in any form or by any electronic,
mechanical, or other means, now known or hereafter
invented, including photocopying and recording, or in any
information storage or retrieval system, without permission in
writing from the publishers.

British Library Cataloguing in Publication Data
A catalogue record for this book is available from the British Library.

Library of Congress Cataloging in Publication Data
Dean, Joan.
  Managing the secondary school/Joan Dean. – 2nd ed.
  p. cm.
  Includes bibliographical references (p. 243).
  ISBN 0–415–08771–6
  1. High schools – Great Britain – Administration. 2. High school
  principals – Great Britain. I. Title.
  LB2822.3.G7D4   1993
  373.12′00941 – dc20   93-13075
                                                              CIP

ISBN 0–415–08771–6

Contents

Figures

Foreword

This is the fourth of Joan Dean's books to be published by Routledge in the education management series. *Managing the Primary School* (1987) and *Special Needs in the Secondary School: the whole school approach* (1989) have been particularly welcomed in schools; and her most recent book *Inspecting and Advising* (1992) is a valuable acquisition to the series at a time when both aspects are in the throes of radical change.

Managing the Secondary School was first published in 1985 by Croom Helm, an imprint now taken over by Routledge. This second edition is not a mere updating but a thorough revision which takes account of the major changes that two major education acts and a host of directives have given rise to in the interim.

Eight years on it is evident that Joan Dean retains her deep concern that school management involves all the teachers in the school, not an élite of senior staff. The materials that she offers in the book have been well tested and clearly will be invaluable in helping teachers understand their roles. Most of the practical work can be undertaken individually, though more will doubtless be gained if teachers share and compare their findings.

Above all, this is not a book that 'lays down the law'. Its wisdom lies in the opportunities it provides for schools and teachers to improve their own managerial practices within the context of the conditions under which they operate.

Cyril Poster

Chapter 1

Leadership and management

The Concise Oxford Dictionary defines the word *lead* in many ways but the following definitions have relevance to leadership in school: 'to cause to go with one, especially by guiding or showing the way or by going in front'; 'to bring to a certain position or destination'.

It defines *management* as: 'the professional administration of business concerns, public undertakings, etc.'.

A headteacher is both a leader and a manager, guiding people to an agreed destination and organising so that it is possible to get there.

Leadership and management in schools today are not easy. The legislation of the past few years has increased the load of head-teachers and senior staff very significantly and they are under pressure from many sources. There are unending demands upon time and energy and there are times when the load is very heavy. Fortunately there are other times when things seem to go well and a headteacher can begin to feel that his or her work has actually made a difference to the learning of students.

Being a leader means knowing where one is going and working to achieve a shared vision with colleagues. Being a manager means getting things done which lead to the realisation of the vision through other people. One criterion by which managers might be judged is their effectiveness in delegating tasks and enabling others to carry them to a successful conclusion.

The word 'manager', used in the context of education, is com-paratively new. Yet it is in many ways descriptive of what is involved. Good management means working with people and resources as they are and helping them to work together to agreed ends. The skilled manager looks for ways in which the interests and abilities of each individual can contribute to the good of the whole and he or she tries to create an organisation and a climate in which this can happen.

There is a good deal known about management which has relevance for schools. Fayol, a mining engineer, suggested that management had five elements – forecasting and planning, organisation, command, coordination and control (Fayol 1949). He also pointed out that there are two kinds of authority: that which derives from the office held and that which derives from personal ability and experience; both are needed for successful management. Authority is the power to issue instructions and obtain compliance with them. Responsibility automatically rests where authority is exercised.

This is evident and relevant in schools. Headteachers and senior staff have authority in the simple sense defined above because of the office they hold, but their effectiveness depends a good deal on their personal experience and abilities.

There is a built-in responsibility for others in any management role, which in schools is not only a supervisory responsibility, but essentially a responsibility for supporting the people for whom one is responsible.

Effective leadership

Being a good leader and manager in school or elsewhere is more than being good at the job being managed. A person may be an excellent classroom teacher but a poor head of department or headteacher. Skill in the classroom may at first win the respect of other staff but unless he or she acquires skill in leading a group of adults, this respect will be dissipated all too rapidly.

All leaders have to live with other people's view of their role. The people responsible to any leader or manager have expectations about the way that person ought to behave and will exert pressure to persuade him or her to conform to their views. Leaders and managers have to reconcile these views with their own view of their role, remembering that initially confidence is engendered when a person behaves in expected ways.

Good leaders select carefully the issues over which they are prepared to take unusual and sometimes unpopular steps. It is not a sign of strength to insist when everyone is passionately opposed to what is being suggested. It often means that those concerned spend a great deal of time grumbling when they might be doing something more positive. It is often a matter of waiting for the right moment to introduce a change.

The ability to lead is sometimes seen as a quality of personality which someone either does or does not possess. There is a notion of truth in this and some brilliant leaders have achieved success because of personal charisma and the vision they set before their followers. Leadership is not exercised in the abstract, however, but in the performance of specific tasks which are mainly those of management. People may find it easier to perform these tasks if they have certain personal qualities and these qualities may be cultivated to some extent, but it may be more profitable to consider the skills and knowledge needed to perform specific leadership tasks effectively and to concentrate on these. It is not unusual to develop appropriate personality traits for the job by cultivating the skills needed to perform the tasks involved.

In most organisations today, leadership is no longer an individual and perhaps autocratic matter, but is to some extent a group activity, with the personal qualities of individual members of the group complementing each other and with some responsibilities delegated or shared. This still leaves the person at the top as the overall leader but one who exercises leadership well will be supported by senior colleagues. This reduces the pressure on the individual and in sharing the tasks of leadership the leader is preparing others to assume those tasks in their turn.

What is involved in being a good manager or leader? The DES paper on school development plans (1991) notes that the headteacher plays the most important role in getting management right. It suggests that this is likely to be most effective when the headteacher:

- has a mission for the school
- inspires commitment to the school's mission, and so gives direction and purpose to its work
- coordinates the work of the school by allocating roles and delegating responsibilities
- is actively and visibly involved in planning and implementing change, but
- is ready to delegate and to value the contribution of colleagues
- is a skilled communicator, keeping everyone informed about important decision and events
- has the capacity to stand back from daily life in order to challenge what is taken for granted, to anticipate problems and spot opportunities

- is committed to the school, its members and its reputation, but
- objectively appraises strengths and weaknesses so as to build upon the best of current practices in remedying deficiencies
- emphasises the quality of teaching and learning, lesson by lesson and day by day
- has high expectations of all staff and all students
- recognises that support and encouragement are needed for everyone to give of their best

There are a number of ways of looking at the tasks of management and leadership. The DES booklets on development planning (1989, 1991) stress the need for evaluation or audit, then planning, then action with these three repeated in a cycle each year or more frequently if necessary.

The successful leader supports individuals and makes them feel of value. This involves discussion with members of a team and a policy of encouragement which may be critical in a supportive way. It is all too easy as headteacher of a large school to encourage some people and miss others. The headteacher's word of encouragement is important to all teachers and other staff as well as to students and it is a good idea to try to be systematic about this to ensure that no one is missed.

A team is formed of individuals and will be successful only if the individuals learn to work together. A secondary school has a great many small teams as well as being one large team and all the teams need to learn to work together. The leader's task is to encourage the feeling of belonging to a team, of mutual trust, support and cooperation.

The support of individuals and of the team is undertaken in order to perform tasks. This gives purpose to the activity and provides criteria for judging success. The overall task for the school is the learning and development of the students, but individual teams need their own specific tasks and part of the planning process involves seeing that these are identified.

Charles Handy suggests that there are four sets of influencing factors which a leader must take into consideration:

- The leader's own preferred style and personal characteristics.
- The preferred style of leadership by the subordinates in the light of circumstances.
- The task, its objectives and technology.

- The environment, the organisational setting, the group and the importance of the task.

He suggests a 'best fit' approach with the view that leadership will be most effective when the requirements of the leader, the subordinates and the task fit together (Handy 1976).

Studies of effective leadership in schools

All researches about effectiveness must start by considering how to define what is effective. The basic criteria are what happens to the students in the school and how well they perform. A great deal is involved in this. The effective headteacher or senior member of staff has to work through other people, so effectiveness in this case will also be concerned with ability to manage and motivate people and to organise the work of the school, so that the students achieve as well as possible.

The question about effective leadership is strongly linked to what is known about effective schools. A good deal of research has been done in this field and most of it stresses the importance of the quality of the leadership. Fullan and Steigelbauer, for example, identify four factors underlying successful improvement processes in schools:

- a feel for the improvement process on the part of leadership;
- a guiding value system;
- intense interaction and communication;
- collaborative planning and implementation.

They state that: 'The effective school effects change (i.e. development) effectively. It establishes a development culture; it is ready for both change (and the learning through dissonance that goes with it) and the release of creative synergy' (Fullan and Steigelbauer 1991).

Reid *et al.*, describing a school improvement project, thought the following eight factors to be characteristic of the effective school:

- curriculum focused leadership;
- supportive climate in the school;
- emphasis on curriculum and instruction;
- clear goals and high expectation for students;
- a system for monitoring performance and achievement;

- on-going staff development and in-service training;
- parental involvement and support;
- LEA support.

(Reid *et al.* 1987)

Mortimore *et al.* in a study of London junior schools found that the length of time a headteacher had been in post was significant in relation to the effectiveness of the school. Headteachers were at their most effective in their influence on students' progress when they had been in the school between three and eleven years (Mortimer *et al.* 1988). This finding may not apply in the much more complex organisation of the secondary school but it seems possible that a similar pattern may exist, with perhaps a longer period before a new headteacher begins to have an effect and possibly a longer period before he or she become less effective.

Overall the researches seem to suggest that the effective school has an effective headteacher who works collaboratively with the staff, sharing with them a·vision of where the school is going and placing emphasis on achievement. Many studies seem to show that the school 'culture' is important for effectiveness.

A paper by Hallinger and Murphy suggests that effective North American schools operate differently according to the social background of their students. Schools with students whose background is of high socio-economic status are supported in their expectations of students by the expectations of parents. Where the background of students is of low socio-economic status this is not so and the school has to set its own expectations (Hallinger and Murphy 1986). In this context the effective principal was forceful in establishing high expectations and standards and there was much use of rewards for students using devices like exhibitions of 'students of the month' and frequent use of assemblies and honour rolls and public lists which recognised academic achievement, improvement, citizenship, attendance and behaviour. This was not needed in the schools with high socio-economic background.

The headteacher also works on the boundary of the school, interacting with those outside it and relating what happens within to the outside. Effectiveness in a headteacher must therefore also be concerned with the ability to manage the boundary. This has become much more important with the changed role of governors stemming from the 1988 Education Act. Managing the boundary means learning to work with governors so that they really contribute to the school and feel part of it. Managing the boundary from other points of view may mean controlling it so that the school benefits from the good effects of what is outside and is protected from the adverse effects.

Effectiveness as a leader might be defined more broadly in terms of the ability to draw together a community of people in pursuit of common goals. It involves inspiring, stimulating, motivating, directing and influencing as well as providing an organisation which supports the work in hand. The effective leader draws together the parts of the organisation and ensures that they all contribute to shared aims.

Other studies are concerned with power and influence. Isherwood (1973) confirms that positional power is important in schools. Rosemary Stewart develops this when she says: 'A wise manager knows the limits of his own authority and, as far as possible, avoids weakening his authority by trying to exercise it where it is likely to be challenged or ignored' (Stewart 1967).

When a person first takes on a managerial role it is not easy to assess and come to terms with the positional power of the new post. Sometimes people under-estimate the effect of the new authority and may be surprised that suddenly, since promotion, their words and actions have an added weight. Conversely, some people over-estimate what the new role allows them to do in over-riding the views and ideas of others. In fact any position allows a person to do certain things but the trust and confidence of colleagues must be won in order to do others. New managers will be wise to fulfil people's expectations of someone holding their post before attempting to do much which is new and unusual.

The power vested in those in leadership roles is bound up to some extent with their ability to provide sticks and carrots as a result of the executive power vested in the office. Headteachers now have greater influence over salaries and promotion than formerly, but there are many other forms of reward which are important to people, including praise and encouragement, the offer of additional responsibilities, the chance to shine, and additional resources, together with the converse of disapproval and withdrawal of opportunities. The evidence generally suggests that reward is more effective than punishment for adults as well as children.

The National Association of Secondary School Principals paper describes studies concerned with leadership behaviour which identify six important leadership functions:

- develop goals, policies and directions
- organise the school and design programmes to accomplish the goals
- monitor progress, solve problems and maintain order
- procure, manage and allocate resources
- create a climate for personal and professional growth and development
- represent the school to the district office and the outside world
(NASSP 1982)

Caldwell and Spinks describe the findings of a study of the use of resources in a school in Tasmania and give five characteristics of the effective school:

1 There is a high degree of involvement of staff in the development of school goals.
2 There are high levels of teacher involvement in decision making in the school.
3 There are high levels of community involvement in decision making in the school.
4 There are high levels of cohesiveness and team spirit among teachers.
5 There is opportunity for appropriate involvement of staff, students and the community in the process of resource allocation.

(Caldwell and Spinks 1988)

The NASSP paper quoted above stressed the value of a high level of expectation on the part of the principal:

In high achieving schools, principals did not let teachers 'write off' students as non-learners particularly because of their race or social class. In low achieving schools the principal helped to depress the teachers' expectations of their students by saying, for example, that they weren't doing too badly for students of their background. Furthermore, the principal's lack of 'push' towards the teacher was carried over into the classroom by teachers who, in turn, expected little of their students.

(NASSP 1982)

They also found that a recurrent characteristic of successful schools was the amount of respect shown to teachers and students. Here the principal set the tone. They found too that where the principal took a strong interest in the quality of teaching this encouraged change and development in teaching methods. Principals also set the tone for discipline in school.

This was confirmed by Rutter *et al.* (1979)who found that in the higher achieving schools the headteacher helped to set the general discipline standards for the whole school. Headteachers set standards by the things they singled out for comment, whether praise or criticism, and by their own behaviour.

The NASSP study also found that successful principals evaluated the work of the school against its agreed goals. In Britain the Education Reform Act (1988) has ensured that evaluation plays a much larger part in the work of teachers and headteachers than it did formerly. The school development plan requires evaluation and there has for some time been a stress on the value of self-evaluation. The DES booklets *Planning for school development* (1989) and *Development planning, a practical guide* (1991) both suggest the need to audit the stage a school has reached as a preliminary to building the development plan.

Marshall and Mitchell found that women were more attuned to curriculum issues, instructional leadership, teachers' concerns, parental involvement, staff development, collaborative planning strategies, community building and the like (Marshall and Mitchell 1989). They concluded that women were more likely to possess characteristics associated with effective leadership in schools than men. This would seem to be an argument for the appointment of more women to leadership positions in this country, too.

Management style

When people move into leadership and management roles in schools, their experience of possible styles of management is usually limited. Most people have seen only a small number of headteachers or senior staff at work and these may represent a limited range of models. The new leader has to apply abilities, personal qualities, views of the role and the circumstances in which she or he is working, to the performance of leadership and management tasks. The particular mixture of approaches and behaviour becomes a style of management which develops slowly as the manager becomes more experienced.

When people first take on management roles, they draw on the models they have known, however unsuitable these may be, because this is all the information they have. A person may copy behaviour observed in others or react against it. As time goes by, each person discovers what works for him or her and, in becoming more confident in the leadership role, gradually develops a style which enables other people to predict his or her reactions. This makes for trusting relationships and makes everyone's work easier, because they do not need to find out what the leader thinks every time they take action.

An aspiring manager needs to study a variety of models, looking for ways of dealing with situations and people and for aspects of management and leadership style which may be appropriate. This means deliberately studying how other people do the job and selecting what seems to the individual to fit, to be a way in which he or she feels it possible to work. Within the school this kind of opportunity should be part of overall staff development for those in middle management.

One way readers can set about the process of working out their own style is to take a hard look at their strengths and limitations, perhaps involving in the process someone with close knowledge of their work. There are many successful ways of leading and managing and how people actually behave in practice is a mixture of their ideas and personality.

A headteacher has to decide how far to be democratic and how far autocratic. The democratic process can be slow and people may become impatient, particularly if they have been used to an autocratic style of leadership. It may, in some circumstances, be better for a person to be more autocratic at the beginning of headship than he or she may wish to be later, if this is what people expect and are used to.

Most schools are gradually moving towards a more collegiate mode of operation and few headteachers now work in isolation. The leadership of schools is usually in the hands of a senior management team rather than a single person. Democratic forms of leadership offer good staff development opportunities, because in order to make a sensible decision a group needs to study the situation carefully. It is also valuable to involve students in some decision making, since part of the school's task is to train young people for life in a democratic society.

It is also necessary to consider which matters can be decided by the headteacher or headteacher and senior staff and which ones require the full involvement of the rest of the staff. In making this decision it should be remembered that one person can have only a limited number of ideas at a time. One benefit of working with others is that it multiplies the ideas available when it comes to making a decision.

People differ in the extent to which they like to work out why they should follow a particular course of action. Many leaders make very good decisions by hunch or intuition, which is perhaps another name for sensitivity to others and to the situation. There is, nevertheless, a need today for a clear rationale both for what the school as a whole is doing and for different parts of its work. Too much is questioned by students, parents, governors and the community for decisions to be arrived at without clear reasoning behind them. People holding senior posts in a school should be able to support practice with theoretical explanations or reasoned argument. They also need to have some kind of theoretical frame of reference in order to be able to judge new developments. On the other hand, it is all too easy, if your mind works that way, to spend a lot of time theorising and be unable to put the theory into practice. A balance is needed.

All good leaders need intuition in making decisions. It is not easy to describe what is meant by the term, but it would seem to have something to do with the sensitivity to people and situations mentioned earlier. It is the kind of sensitivity which leads a person to sense the best thing to do at a level below that of conscious thought. When in doubt it is usually best to take time to think things through although it must be remembered that people find it extremely difficult to live with uncertainty. Intuition is something to be cultivated but it should be checked by reason.

A person whose vision is strong needs to be careful to pay enough attention to the ideas of others. Leaders who find that no one else seems to have ideas should be suspicious about what they are doing when ideas are offered. When a leader first takes up a new appointment people may be slow to offer ideas, but if they go on being slow, it is probably the leader's fault. One of the tasks of management is to help everyone to be more fluent in having ideas and carrying them through.

A slightly different problem is when a leader has very good ideas. If he or she doesn't limit those offered at any one time or limit them to those people who can take them, others will start to take the view that 'it isn't any use the rest of us thinking of things because he/she is sure to have a much better idea'.

This isn't an easy situation for a leader. Sometimes it will be necessary to stand back and watch people struggling through to the idea he or she started off with. Sometimes the leader will realise that by speaking instead of keeping quiet, he or she has stifled a possible idea before it came to birth.

The tasks and skills of management

The Post Project, the study of the appointment of secondary school headteachers (Morgan *et al.* 1983) found that most appointing committees were inclined to consider the personality of candidates rather than their skills and experience of the tasks involved in headship. This is familiar to many people who have been involved in the appointment of headteachers and others. Adjectives like 'hard-working', 'enthusiastic', are likely to be used in discussing candidates along with phrases like 'intellectually able', 'makes good relationships', 'strong personality' and so on. Interviewing panels will also be considering the appropriateness of an individual's experience, knowledge and competence, but when the decision is being made, qualities of personality are well to the fore as criteria. This has changed a little in some areas as a result of the Post Project, but governing bodies are now responsible for the appointment of headteachers and unless they contain people used to industrial methods of appointment, may still place most emphasis on personality.

This is, of course, a very proper concern in making an appointment. The personality of a headteacher is crucial to his or her success but it should not be the only criterion. Appointing committees need to remember that any managerial post involves the ability to undertake specific tasks and the appointing committee needs to ensure that the successful candidate has experience of a number of these tasks and has the kind of approach and skill which will enable him or her to learn how to cope with new ones.

When a teacher is appointed to a post of responsibility the appointing committee has to judge whether a candidate possesses or will be able to learn the skills to perform successfully in the new role. The judgement for middle management posts may have to be based on the teacher's performance in the classroom which may or may not be a good predictor of ability to manage adults. In more senior posts candidates will have experience of managing adults and the selection procedure should find out how successfully each candidate was able to do this.

It is perhaps easier to make judgements about this if one starts from the tasks involved in a given post and considers the skill and knowledge likely to be required for their successful performance. This kind of analysis is also useful in training people for posts of responsibility and may provide an opportunity for self-assessment for those aspiring to senior posts.

The precise nature and distribution of management tasks may vary from one school to another and different people will undertake them in different ways, but the broad outline of the tasks at each level is roughly similar.

The list shown in Figure 1.1 outlines some of the tasks of leadership and management. These are not all tasks for the headteacher but tasks for the senior management of the school. Similar lists could be given for teachers with other levels of responsibility. Management also involves specific skills and those are listed in the last column of the table.

The development of the ability to undertake these tasks and the acquisition of the necessary knowledge and skills for management is an extension of the skills teachers have already started to acquire in the classroom. Some of them simply need development in a different context. This should be a continuous process so that by the time people achieve a headship, they are already competent in most of the work involved. Management ability is best acquired through a gradual increase in the responsibilities teachers undertake, preferably with many opportunities to work with expert and experienced colleagues and to talk over performance and progress.

Skill and knowledge can also be acquired as part of a training scheme and individuals can do much to improve their own performance by observing others at work and by trying out ideas.

Conclusion

Analysing the tasks of management makes them appear separate – a collection of processes taking place in the same context. In practice it is not like that. The pieces of the puzzle are part of a whole. One is never dealing with only one thing at a time, but each action and situation contains growth possibilities for a number of goals. One has to become skilled at recognising and using situations as they arise.

	Tasks	Skills
Aims, objectives, policies	Articulate aims for the school	Presentation Communication Negotiation Leading discussion Decision making Evaluation Planning Timetabling
	Ensure that aims are considered	
	Articulate and implement policies	
Sch devt plan	Draw up the school development plan	
The curriculum	Articulate the curriculum philosophy of the school	
	Ensure that the National Curriculum is implemented	
	Ensure professional standards of performance	
	Maintain oversight of continuity	
	Maintain an overview and encourage coherence	
Organisation	Organise the school effectively for teaching and learning	
	Ensure that there are equal opportunities for all students	
	Deploy staff and other resources effectively	
	Provide a timetable	

Figure 1.1 The tasks and skills of management

	Tasks	Skills
Managing change	Manage change effectively	Presentation Communication Negotiation Evaluation Decision making Discussion leadership Survey skills Public relations Marketing Administration Financial management
	Manage decision making effectively	
	Plan effectively	
Marketing the school	Survey the views of students and parents	
	Analyse strengths, weaknesses, opportunities, threats	
	Set objectives for public relations	
	Organise the marketing of the school	
School administration	Oversee the administrative work of the school	
	Control the school finances	
	Be responsible for buildings and environment	
	Ensure conformity with health and safety legislation	
Pastoral care and discipline	Establish philosophy of care and discipline	
	Create and maintain a system for pastoral care	
	Create and maintain a system for discipline	
	Ensure the personal and social development of all students	
	Create and maintain record keeping systems	

Figure 1.1 (Continued)

	Tasks	Skills
Managing people	Lead and motivate staff	Consultation Motivation Delegation Decision making Problem solving Negotiation Communication Presentaion Interviewing Administration Appraisal
	Delegate effectively	
	Deal effectively with staff problems	
	Have knowledge of relevant legislation	
Communication	Ensure appropriate communication for everyone	
	Create and maintain communication systems	
	Ensure that information travels in all directions	
	Seek feedback from all levels	
	Evaluate the effectiveness of communication	
Staff selection and development	Organise and assist with staff appointments	
	Establish policy for staff development and appraisal	
	Create a development programme for all staff	
	Evaluate the staff development programme	
	Maintain records for staff and provide any necessary reports	

Figure 1.1   (Continued)

	Tasks	Skills
School and community	Represent the school to the outside world	Communication Presentation Evaluation
	Support governors in developing their work	
	Involve parents where appropriate	
	Establish relationships with employers	
	Encourage the use of the community for learning	
Evaluation and assessment	Establish a policy for assessment and evaluation	
	Ensure regular evaluation of the school	

Figure 1.1   (Continued)

Analysis also implies a beginning and an end to developments and tasks. In practice the development of a school or a person is a slowly evolving process which is continuous. Plans for development change as growth takes place and the original pattern becomes something more and new goals emerge. People change and develop and create new possibilities. And as teams develop they enlarge the experience and possibilities of their members.

Growth involves both new experience and the ability to see past experience in a new way. It is the task of the leader to enlarge the experience of those he or she leads.

Among the most important characteristics in leaders is a belief in themselves and in those they lead – a belief that everyone is in the process of growing and developing.

Chapter 2

Aims, objectives and policies

Aims

Any judgement about the effectiveness of a particular organisation depends upon what that organisation is attempting to do. A school has a very complex set of aims, because it is not only attempting to give students knowledge and skills but is also concerned with their socialisation, their moral behaviour, their attitudes and much else besides. In addition it is concerned with the adults in the school community. A school is a learning place for everyone who works there.

The management tasks involved in developing aims, objectives and policies are as follows:

1 Articulate aims for the school.
2 Ensure that aims are considered and objectives are formulated.
3 Articulate and implement policies.

Articulate aims for the school

Every school now has to make a statement about its aims and publish them for the benefit of parents and other interested members of the public. If the aims are to be to the forefront of the thinking of governors and staff and to some extent of parents and students, then there is a need for their involvement in arriving at these aims and revising them on a regular basis. Only new schools will be concerned about articulating aims for the first time. For most schools it will be a matter of reviewing aims annually in relation to the school development plan and various policies and documents.

In this context it may be helpful to consider a number of criteria in relation to the school aims. It is suggested that schools should be concerned with students:

- learning within the National Curriculum;
- having concern for equal opportunities for all;
- preparing for life in a multi-cultural, multi-lingual world and for closer links with Europe;
- developing the skills of communication, numeracy, study, problem-solving, personal and social behaviour and information technology;
- having economic and industrial understanding;
- preparing for adult life through careers education;
- developing concern for their own health through health education;
- preparing for adult life through education in citizenship;
- developing concern for the environment;
- acquiring a framework of meaning for life and a value system;
- acquiring knowledge of religions;
- developing positive attitudes.

A school also needs to have aims for adults and for its relationship with parents and with the community. The following areas need to be developed:

- the work of teachers and other adults;
- the school's public image;
- relationships with parents;
- relationships with contributory schools;
- relationships with schools, colleges and other institutions to which students proceed;
- relationships with employers who accept students for work experience and as employees;
- relationships with the local community.

In addition, the school will need a programme of improvement to the school building and environment and for the purchase of equipment. This will be part of the School Development Plan.

Ensure that aims are considered and objectives are formulated

If these aims are to be part of everyone's thinking about the school there will be a need to consider how this is achieved. When aims are initially arrived at, everyone can be involved in considering them, but as time goes on those who were initially involved may forget the experience and new people will have joined who were not part of the original discussion. The school needs to have ways of building consideration of aims into its work so that people are constantly aware of them.

One way of doing this is to ask that plans each year from each department show how the work is related to the school aims. The School Development Plan itself must show this, and this will help people to keep aware of the aims. It may be a good idea to put them in the governors' report to parents each year so that parents are kept aware of what the school is setting out to do. In short, every opportunity for reminding people of the school's aims needs to be taken.

Aims need to be turned into objectives which in turn become plans for work. These will be part of the School Development Plan and part of the plans of each department or faculty within the school.

Articulate and implement policies

Aims and objectives are closely linked with policies. A policy might be described as a statement of the behaviour expected in a given context. Schools need to make policies explicit, setting them down as a statement of guidance for staff or students and attempting to establish a normal way of working in given circumstances. Policy statements need to be part of the staff handbook so that all staff are aware of them and some of the statements will be part of the school prospectus.

Just as aims need to be discussed with everyone concerned when they are being formed, so policies need to involve all staff and governors and sometimes parents.

Policy statements will vary according to the subject in question but are likely to contain statements such as the following:

- the overall philosophy and principles operating in the area in question;
- the attitudes expected;
- the roles of those concerned;
- specific arrangements needed;
- the organisation of any material resources or equipment;
- methods of reviewing progress and recording where appropriate;
- the support available to teachers;
- relevant staff development;

– the place of any links with contributory schools or transfer schools and colleges.

Policies will be needed in each major area of school life. The following are suggested:

Curriculum

- what is to be taught at each level, taking the National Curriculum into account;
- how the most and least able are to be dealt with;
- teaching methods;
- homework;

There will also be a need for policy statements for each aspect of curriculum. These should be the responsibility of the appropriate head of department.

Organisation

- the way students are grouped for learning, the use of time and space and the reasoning behind the organisation;
- staff responsibilities and relationships;
- the communication system;
- the organisation of the school office;

Planning and decision making

- the way the School Development Plan is built up;
- the role of teaching and other staff in overall planning;
- the decision making patterns;
- the way finance is dealt with;

Pastoral care and discipline

- what is expected of teachers by way of pastoral care;
- how problems are to be dealt with;
- the guidance offered to students about courses and careers;
- the system of student records;
- the discipline system and how it is to be applied;

Assessment and evaluation

- what is to be assessed and how;
- the part that assessment and evaluation play in the life of the school;
- the way students' work and behaviour are assessed;
- the way teachers and other staff are assessed and the appraisal system;

Community relationships

- relationships with the governing body;
- relationships with parents;
- relationships with employers;
- relationships with the local community;
- relationships with other schools and colleges;
- public relations;

Equal opportunities

- for boys and girls;
- for students of different ethnic groups;
- for students with disabilities;
- for students of different social backgrounds;

Staff development

- overall philosophy;
- organisation for staff development;
- needs assessment;
- the way the staff development programme is built up;
- evaluation of the staff development programme;

Staff selection

- the system used to select staff.

Policies have to be implemented by the whole staff and they represent the values and vision of the school. It is therefore important that staff are involved in their development. This can provide a valuable form of in-service work for many teachers. The extent to which a headteacher devolves the writing of policies depends a good deal on the stage a school has reached in its development. There will be situations where the staff will find the vision of a headteacher newly in post very foreign and the new incumbent will therefore be hesitant about spending time writing policies. In this situation it may be best for the headteacher to produce basic policies in essential areas to stand until the staff are ready to go further.

There are also other groups which may need to be consulted about policies. For example, parents will have views about the school's communication and it may be a good idea to gather a small group of parents to discuss what they would like by way of communication about their children's progress and about the work of the school generally. Similarly a headteacher has to decide what it is important to tell governors.

Parents may also have valuable contributions to make about the pastoral care and discipline systems. If home and school act together on discipline, both are likely to be more effective.

Chapter 3

The school development plan

Draw up the school development plan

All schools are now required to produce a development plan. This has made standard procedure something which good schools have been doing for a long time and most LEAs have provided documents to help schools with this process. The DES has also published two useful papers on the school development plan (1989, 1991).

There is a great deal of evidence from research into effectiveness in school which shows that effective schools work collaboratively (Little 1982, Reynolds (ed.) 1985, Reid *et al.* 1987, Mortimore *et al.* 1988, Beare *et al.* 1989). The school development plan offers a particular opportunity for everyone to work together to contribute. It is worth setting aside at least one inset day for looking at ways in which the thinking through of departmental and other plans contributes to the school plan. Most writing about School Development Plans suggests that there is a cycle of reviewing the situation, planning, implementing and evaluating and then going through the same process again the following year, building on the work already done. Plans also need to be both long-term and short-term, planning some things for the coming year and others on a three- or four-year prediction. While the massive changes which have been coming into education do not encourage head-teachers and governors to plan for the long term, there is nevertheless value in planning broadly and adapting plans as developments take place.

Reviewing the situation

Most schools will now be in the position of having worked through development plans and will have undertaken an initial major review. The task then is to identify the best way to review annually without making this too large a task. If the school has undergone inspection since the last development plan was drawn up, this will provide material for the revised plan. A good way forward would seem to be first to identify from the previous year those areas which have shown themselves to be clearly in need of review and then to consider whether there are new areas which should also be considered. The list shown in Figure 3.1 may help in determining areas which should be investigated. One useful way of using this list would be to ask each member of staff to complete it, perhaps working on a departmental or other group basis.

The DES publication (1989) on school development plans stresses that it is important to set the audit of the school in the context of its aims and values. A basic question is 'Have we achieved our aims?'. It is also important to consider whether the school is meeting the policies and initiatives of central and local government.

The second DES publication (1991) suggests that selecting areas for audit is done by the governors on the advice of the headteacher and that carrying out the audit is the responsibility of one teacher or a team working with the headteacher. The intention of the team is not that it does all the work. Everyone needs to have some involvement, but the team is responsible for organising the review.

The areas chosen for review should be fairly limited, with the idea that the school looks at everything over a period of several years. The plan can then be adapted year by year. There will always be areas which suggest themselves as being particularly in need of attention.

The next task is to consider priorities among the areas selected. Some may not be all that urgent and could be put into the plan for a future year. Other priorities may be treated together where there is common ground among them.

Once the areas for review have been selected the team is then responsible for organising the next stage. The review will be in a number of different pieces, as each group of staff looks at its particular responsibilities, and these need to be drawn together. This could be a task for the team, although the DES paper (1991) suggests that it is a task for the headteacher or for a senior member of the staff. The same paper also stresses the value of getting an external view. This will, in the first place, come from the governors, but could also come from external advisers.

School analysis	++	+	av	−	− −
Core and foundation subjects and RE English Mathematics Modern languages Science Technology History Geography Art Music Physical education Religious education					
Skills communication numeracy study problem solving personal and social information technology					
Themes economic and industrial understanding careers education and guidance health education education for citizenship environmental education					
Dimensions Equal opportunities for boys and girls students of different races students of different abilities students of different social backgrounds students with disabilities Multicultural education European education World education					

Figure 3.1 School analysis

School analysis	++	+	av	–	– –
Curriculum continuity year to year teacher to teacher primary to secondary school on from secondary school					
Overall organisation teacher deployment grouping for learning provision for most able students provision for least able students					
Use of time timetable arrangements use of time by teachers use of time by students use of time by office staff use of time by other staff time spent on different activities					

Resources
provision and use of
   books
   equipment
   information technology
   space					

Arrangements for planning and decision making effectiveness involvement of staff involvement of students involvement of governors involvement of parents					

Figure 3.1 (Continued)

School analysis	+ +	+	av	–	– –
Effectiveness of pastoral care system Role of form teacher Students' attitudes and behaviour Control of truancy Discipline system					
Effectiveness of student record keeping Involvement of students in their records Maintenance of records Use of records					

Effectiveness of day to day running of
school
    arrangements for lunch
    arrangements for assembly
    arrangements for break times
    arrangements for wet breaks
    staff duties					

Effectiveness of administration
    work of office staff
    financial planning
    accounting
    arrangements for odering goods and
        equipment
    correspondence					

Environment
    quality of environment
    cleanliness
    state of repair
    arrangements for dealing with
        maintenance
    state of grounds
    arrangements for grounds maintenance
    students' care of the environment					

Figure 3.1   (Continued)

School analysis	++	+	av	–	– –

Communication of head and senior management with
    teaching staff
    other staff
    students
    governors
    parents
    contributory schools
    continuing schools/colleges
    local industry/employers
    community
    LEA
Communication among staff
Communication from students
Communication from parents
Communication of staff with governors
Communication of staff with parents					

Staff performance
    senior management
    middle management
    classroom teachers					

Staff selection and development
    arrangements for staff selection
    arrangements for needs assessment
    induction of new staff
    support for newly qualified teachers
    staff development programme
    inset days
    arrangements for appraisal
    staff records					

Figure 3.1   (Continued)

School analysis	++	+	av	−	−−
Relationships with 　parents 　governors 　LEA 　contributory schools 　transfer schools/colleges 　neighbourhood and community 　local industry/employers Public image of the school Arrangements for public relations Number of students putting the school as first choice					
Arrangements for evaluating 　overall curriculum 　curriculum materials 　teaching approaches 　match of curriculum to individuals Individual progress Record keeping Internal tests, examinations External examination results					
Arrangements for evaluating 　organisation for learning 　day-to-day organisation 　general administration 　financial administration 　pastoral care 　discipline 　planning 　communication 　staff selection 　staff development 　appraisal 　evaluation systems					

Figure 3.1   (Continued)

Making the plan

The next task is to make plans for each of the areas identified. Many of the areas chosen will fall naturally to particular groups to develop. Departmental reviews, for example, should lead to departmental teams defining their own objectives and plans. Other areas may be the province of senior staff. Some small tasks might be allocated to individuals.

It will be important to create a school framework for planning so that each contribution fits the overall plan. This framework should indicate how the plan should be set out. A possible list might include statements about:

- aims and objectives
- performance criteria
- plans for achieving the objectives
- implications for staff development
- the implementation plan
- responsibilities for parts of the programme
- cost in time and money
- evaluation of the programme

Each stage of the implementation plan needs to be worked out. One useful way of doing this is to use network analysis. This involves writing down the major 'events' in the plan. These are activities which happen at a point in time, such as:

- the publication of a discussion paper outlining problems which need to be tackled
- a meeting to discuss the paper with a group of staff
- agreement about some action

This will provide material to start the analysis.

The next task is to set out on paper a number of circles divided across the centre. An event is written in the top half of each circle, and the bottom part, which is divided into two, gives the earliest and latest dates by which each event might take place (see Figure 3.2). Between the events there will be action, sometimes several different actions running concurrently. Actions are represented by lines joining the events. These should be entered before the dates are set because the amount of time needed will depend upon how much there is to be done between events.

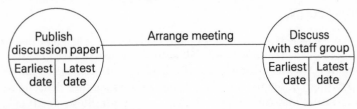

Figure 3.2 Network analysis

Lastly the dates should be entered. The finalising of dates may need to be left until the whole development plan is brought together so that different parts of it can be planned in sequence, but proposed dates should be entered on the network. Dates may then need to be modified so that not too much is taking place at the same time with the same people.

Network planning is very useful as a group method of working, using a flip-chart to set out the steps which need to be taken. It has the additional advantage that networks for different programmes can be placed side by side to see how they relate to each other. Each part of the programme needs to be the responsibility of individuals or groups. It should be quite clear what each person is expected to do.

It is essential to know what the plans suggested will cost and to re-draw them until they are within the budget. It may be helpful to groups to be given a target sum for their planning with the possibility of negotiating for more if it seems necessary. This will help all teachers to be aware of the school's finances.

Thought should also be given to the time involved in any plan. Teachers' time is not elastic and there are already enormous demands upon it. If time is considered in planning there is some hope that plans will be realistic. It may also be a matter of time-tabling so that time is made for some people to undertake development work.

Evaluation should always be considered at the planning stage. The following should be decided:

- how the evaluation will be done
- when it will be done, including ways in which information about the success of the programme can be collected as the work takes place
- who will be responsible for it
- what kind of reporting will be needed

Once all the sections of the plans have been set out, they need to be drawn together to make an overall plan. The overall plan needs checking to see that time is sensibly planned, that not too much is expected to happen at the same time and that costs are realistic. Some groups may need to postpone plans or parts of plans until a later year.

Implementing the plan

Once the plans have been agreed by the staff and by the governors they can be implemented. If each group involved has allocated responsibilities adequately this should simply be a matter of starting work on what has been planned. The Surrey Education Department paper (1990) suggests a number of key questions which might be considered at this stage:

1   Are individuals clear about their responsibilities in implementing the plan?
2   Are the deadlines, time scales and budgetary implications clearly understood by all?
3   Are success criteria (performance indicators) set for each person and each task?
4   Who will monitor the outcome?

Evaluating the outcomes

Each group involved in the planning needs to consider evaluation so that this can go forward alongside the work planned. There should be provision for monitoring the programme as it proceeds and each part of the plan should be the specific responsibility of one individual. Monitoring might involve discussing the progress of the plan regularly with individuals, observing work in progress, checking on student performance, looking at records and so on. Decisions need to be made at the planning stage about the frequency of the monitoring and its cost in terms of time. More detailed information about methods of evaluation is given in Chapter 16.

There is also a need to evaluate the overall success of the plan. It will be important to consider whether the work planned was too much or too little; whether the devolution of responsibilities worked effectively; whether the monitoring and evaluation were effective; how far objectives have been achieved; whether the staff development programme was adequate to support the developments planned; whether the work done has affected students' performance.

Chapter 4

Students

Development

Secondary school students are at their most problematic stage of development. Western society, unlike some primitive cultures, has no particular point at which boys and girls become regarded as men and women. The points at which a person becomes physically adult, may leave school, drive a car, vote, are all different and the transition from childhood to adulthood is a long and uncertain one, during which the young person has the task of adjusting to the very different expectations that we have for adults compared with those for children. The fact that most young people are physically adult while they are still in what is regarded as a childhood establishment, a school, is difficult for some.

Many young people also have problems because of the pace of adolescent growth. A boy or girl moves physically from being a child into being a young adult very quickly and for some the adjustment in terms of the behaviour expected is difficult. Adolescence is also the time when self-consciousness reaches a peak and young people are extremely sensitive to other people's views, particularly those of the peer group. One of the most valuable things a school can offer to a young person is a good self-image and the confidence which stems from it, both in his or her ability to learn and in social confidence. This is particularly necessary for those whose home background and ability does not give social confidence or interest in learning. There is a tendency, which is all too understandable, to offer the responsibility needed for the development of social confidence to those who have shown that they can take it, rather than those who need the experience. Social learning needs to be taken seriously as part of the school's contribution to student development. Many young people appear gauche because they do not know how to behave in certain situations.

For some students, home will give them confidence to move in any social circle. Others may be limited by their home background unless the school helps them to widen their horizons. Some young people find the same language spoken at home and at school. Others have had to learn the language of school, even though English is their home language, and this learning persists into the secondary school. The requirement to learn to use standard English is part of the National Curriculum. Still others have had to learn English as a second language. Work on knowledge of language can help students to see that there are many valid ways of expressing oneself and the need is for appropriate language for different situations. Boys, in particular, tend to be inarticulate in adolescence and much work needs to be done to make all students articulate and able to express themselves orally. This is part of being socially self-confident as well as being part of the National Curriculum. It is not just something for the English lesson, or even for lessons generally, but something which needs to be part of the overall life of the school. There should be many situations where students are required to talk socially and express their views, such as greeting visitors and taking them round the school, dealing with parents and other visitors on an open day, inviting guests to lunch and talking to them, talking to employers on work experience. It may be worth recruiting some parents who find it easy to converse with reticent adolescents, to talk to individuals who find conversation difficult, about their interests and work.

Learning

Students coming into the secondary school are at very different stages of development. Some are ready for abstract approaches to learning; others are at a much earlier stage. The Stage 2 SATs tests will, from September 1994, give the secondary school a clearer idea than is offered at present about the stage different students have reached. This will enable teachers more effectively to group children for learning, although it will be important to recognise that there is still variety among students who have reached the same level in the National Curriculum.

In order to learn from the words of others, or even from pictures, it is necessary to be able to call on relevant experience.

Primary schools devote a lot of time to providing first-hand experience, so that the words of the teacher and of books really mean something. The need for this is less evident in the secondary school but teachers still need to be aware that the life experience of students is comparatively limited, yet very varied, and a student who has not experienced something or who has drawn little from an experience, will have an incomplete understanding of explanations in class, however clearly given. This is the reason why field work and practical work in science and mathematics are so important. Teachers introducing new topics in teaching need to start by checking the experience that students have to enable them to understand what is said.

Another problem about teaching is that students may appear to understand what they have learned but be unable to apply this in everyday life. This may be the problem behind some of the complaints from employers that school leavers do not know work which the school has covered on many occasions. This is partly a question of how knowledge is stored in the mind and partly a question of making a bridge between what is learned and its everyday application.

As students grow older and their store of experience and knowledge grows, the way they bank it in their minds becomes important. The framework of subject areas offered by the school in itself provides a method of storing knowledge but brings the problem that students may not see the connections between areas of knowledge, which often need to be made explicitly. Much work needs to be done on sorting out what is known. Planning for essays, displays, preparing for examinations and many other activities in school offer chances for students to sort out their thinking and put it in order and the skills for doing this need to be taught and practised if knowledge is to be usable. A useful way of doing this is described in Novak and Gowin's book *Learning how to Learn* which suggests that students make a concept map of what they know in any area, in a way rather similar to that which primary teachers use for preparing projects (Novak and Gowin 1984). This involves writing down the key points in any area of learning and then looking at how they are connected. This can be a very good way of sorting out thinking in any subject area and has the advantage that the teacher can see quickly where a student's thinking is going astray.

It is also necessary to make a bridge between what is learned in the classroom and its application in daily life. Most work should involve this kind of thinking and every possible opportunity for actually applying learning should be taken. For example, much of the correspondence and telephoning over field work might be done by students under the teacher's supervision and with covering letters where necessary. Preparations for an open day might be done by students to a much greater extent than is common in most schools.

The needs of individuals

A good school is concerned about individual students. Different students will have different needs and the pastoral care system of the school should be prepared to see that the needs of all individuals are met. It is particularly important to see that those with special needs are catered for, including the very able and gifted, not only by special needs teachers but by all staff. A school needs to have a whole school policy for dealing with children with special needs and to see that these are met in every class and not only in special groups. This may mean substantial in-service work for subject teachers. For the head and senior staff, the task is to cater for the needs of these students through the way the school is organised and through the teaching and learning programme.

Staff problems in dealing with individual difficulties

Teachers need support in dealing with the range of students, particularly when they are in mixed ability groups. They may need in-service help in dealing with the range of problems if the school is adopting a whole school approach to special needs. Young and inexperienced teachers may find themselves dealing with students of unfamiliar backgrounds, perhaps of a different ethnic group or social class, and may need help in understanding this. They may also need help in developing the ability to control students in groups.

Another problem which is not confined to inexperienced teachers is the need to treat students according to their age. This is a difficulty which teachers share with parents. People respond to the way they are treated and students treated as children will behave like children. It is important to demonstrate the expectation that they will behave in adult ways and to work accordingly, while still being sympathetic towards lapses in behaviour. This kind of issue needs a lot of staff discussion and consideration of the differences in treatment which should be used as students grow older.

The other difficulty that teachers have in the secondary school is providing for the range of ability which any class represents. It is much easier to do this in the primary school where students are with one teacher for much of the time. This is an issue which departments should be encouraged to consider. Work assignments can gradually be built up so that for each topic taught there are assignments at different levels.

Bullying

A good deal of concern has been expressed recently about bullying in schools and there is evidence (Boulton and Underwood 1992) admittedly in this case from a small number of schools, that a considerable proportion of children are bullied at some stage of their schooling. This may not necessarily be physical: children find name calling and verbal bullying distressing as well. News programmes have also spoken of children bullied because they do not have the clothing which is currently fashionable and in other cases having such clothing stolen. An analysis by Jean La Fontaine (1990) of calls received on Esther Rantzen's Childline suggests that children are intimidated by a far wider range of harassment than adults are aware of.

By the time they reach the secondary school, children are well acquainted with the peer group rule that one does not tell tales. Bullying may therefore go unrecognised by staff until someone is injured or made ill by the treatment he or she is receiving from the peer group or from older boys and girls. The ability to recognise the symptoms and incidence of bullying therefore needs to be included in the school discipline policy and continual care needs to be exercised by staff and encouragement given to students to avoid bullying and to help the staff to deal with it when it arises. All students in the school need to know that bullying is considered unacceptable and that they will be supported if they help to stop it. Work in drama may be valuable here in encouraging students to look at bullying from the victim's point of view. Incidents of bullying should also be recorded so that individuals who are inclined to bully and those who tend to be victims can be watched and supported. There should also be a system for dealing with complaints about bullying from parents and with other cases as they come to light. This problem needs continual vigilance on the part of staff, including those with responsibility for supervision at lunch time and other non-teaching staff as well as teachers. All cases reported must be taken very seriously and regarded not only as an infringement of the rules of the school, but as an infringement of its ethos.

Truancy

Among the data which schools have to make available is the truancy rate. This is likely to put some pressure on schools to do everything they can to keep attendance rates at their peak, especially during the final years at school when some students tend to take time off. A recent survey by NFER showed that 23 per cent of 13-year-olds admitted to having truanted in the previous year and 9 per cent of 11-year-olds were also truanting occasionally. Figures for older students are likely to be worse.

Some schools are now introducing computer-based systems for checking the presence of students not only at the beginning of the day but in each lesson. One of the most effective schemes supplies each student with a plastic card which he or she pushes through an electronic reader to check in each morning and for each lesson. The information is fed into the school computer and absence is checked immediately and can be followed up. Students are fined for lost cards.

Students who are frequently absent from school without excuse are often part of the group of those disenchanted with education. Disenchantment grows with continued failure and it is important for the school to see that as many students as possible succeed in as many areas as possible. Once a student has started taking days off, he or she is likely to fail further because of missing lessons.

Truancy is likely to be less prevalent where there are clear shared goals, commitment to purpose, dedicated teachers, high expectations and collaborative work, active leadership and support, good school organisation and clear policies leading to academic achievement, a rigorous and focused curriculum, a positive and orderly school culture and community relationships. Good schools have fewer truants.

Chapter 5

The curriculum

Any consideration of the tasks of management in schools must have curriculum as a central concern since all the activity of the school is concerned with student learning.

The headteacher and senior staff of the school have responsibility for all aspects of teaching and learning. This involves the following management tasks:

1 Articulate the curriculum philosophy of the school.
2 Ensure that the National Curriculum is implemented.
3 Ensure professional standards of performance.
4 Maintain oversight of continuity.
5 Maintain an overview and encourage coherence.

Articulate the curriculum philosophy of the school

The headteacher must see that there is a curriculum philosophy and a curriculum which is more than the sum of the subjects taught or of the National Curriculum.

Curriculum can be seen in many ways. There is a sense in which all societies educate their young, although it is only relatively recently that this has become a task to be undertaken by people specially trained to do it. Education in every society is concerned with teaching children and young people how to live in that society, whether this is a matter of bare survival or a matter of how to have a good life. There will always be some education in relationships with other people. This may be to do with how to show respect to others, how to work within a group or with the rituals of human relationships. There will also be concern about passing on the culture, including such things as the history of the society, its religion, its systems for living together and its values, attitudes and way of life.

Figure 5.1 The curriculum

Curriculum can be seen from three points of view: that of the child, of the content and of the society (see Figure 5.1). The stress we place on each of these varies with time and place. In a society where education is not a specialist task entrusted to teachers but a matter of adults teaching students to undertake the tasks of everyday living, the curriculum content will be concerned with food, clothing and shelter, hunting or farming skills and the skills and knowledge needed to defend the community and possibly to increase its goods and territory by fighting its neighbours. There may also be stories, legends and myths to be passed on, religious beliefs and rites and ceremonies to be learned. The curriculum, if it can be so called, is about the needs of society.

Once a leisured group emerges in a society and there is time to develop arts and skills for pleasure and to explore knowledge in its own right, a curriculum will be created for the students of this group which is knowledge-based and which gradually becomes more concerned with the passing on of the culture. Thus we see the curriculum as concerned more with content than with society's needs and it may become divorced from them, even to the point of thinking that it is morally superior to be concerned with knowledge for its own sake rather than knowledge for use. These patterns can be seen at many times in history and currently there is a struggle among proponents of all three views of the curriculum.

Any aspect of the curriculum can be seen from these three viewpoints. If we look at mathematics from the point of view of society, our questions are about how adults use mathematics and the mathematics people need in the adult world.

If we consider mathematics from the point of view of the subject itself, we use different criteria. We ask questions about such things as the nature of mathematical knowledge. What forms of language does it use? How do parts of the subject relate to other parts? The answers to questions of this kind help to identify what should be selected for inclusion in the curriculum by considering how the structure of the subject can be built up.

Finally we consider the learner's view. We must then be concerned with the experience needed to understand the material, the development of thinking skills which allow understanding, the use the learners see for what they are learning and the actual way they learn. These considerations enable us to select material for different students, place it in sequence and help them to apply what they are learning. All three of these aspects should be present in the curriculum offered to students and it is a good characteristic of the National Curriculum that for the most part all three aspects are represented.

The National Curriculum is stated largely in terms of content. It is equally important to think of it in terms of process. This is the way in which individuals structure and store knowledge to enable them to draw on it when it is needed. The process by which learning takes place determines how the knowledge is stored and structured and although a teacher can offer students a structure, this is less valuable than the process of actually making the structure oneself. For example, a great deal of work in science in the past has given students hypotheses and dictated the experiments which might be done to confirm them. Modern thinking includes a great deal of work involving students developing hypotheses and working out how to test them. This helps students to structure their thinking in a way which the more formal method could never do.

Yet another way of looking at curriculum lies in the definition adopted. The curriculum has been described as all the intended outcomes of the school. This limits the idea mainly to what happens in classrooms and in classroom-associated activity. But differences between schools are more subtle than this. Some important experiences that students take away from school are not part of the intended outcomes in the same sense as the National Curriculum. David Hargreaves, in his report *Improving Secondary Schools* (1984), and a number of others, speak of the hidden curriculum of values and attitudes conveyed by the way the school operates and the way that adults within it behave. But the hidden curriculum is also divided. There is what might be described as the inferential curriculum – the learning inferred by the students from the way the school is run, the things seen to be valued by staff, the way teachers treat students and the examples given. This is not entirely hidden and some of it is intended.

There is also the true hidden curriculum which by definition is learning which is neither intended nor recognised. As soon as this learning becomes recognised it becomes part of the inferential curriculum, but much will still remain hidden. A school may thus be giving messages which its headteacher and staff would not wish to give and it is a good idea to look at this area occasionally to discover if possible what hidden messages are being transmitted.

The stated curriculum philosophy of the school therefore needs to have reference not only to the intended curriculum, but also to the inferred and the hidden curriculum. The statement about the inferred curriculum is particularly important because it is about values and attitudes and is likely to have a more lasting effect than much else learned at school. Staff need to spend time discussing it and thinking about how values and forms of behaviour are inculcated.

Some of these aims will be the subject of direct teaching. Others will be acquired as part of work in different areas of curriculum. Yet others will be learned as part of the daily life of the school. Students' learning goes on all the time and the way students are treated in school and the expectations about their behaviour affect their attitudes and are part of the learning process. The staff of every school needs to spend time thinking about what students can infer from their treatment and from the daily life of the school.

Ensure that the National Curriculum is implemented

The curriculum a school adopts must first provide opportunity for the relevant learning within the National Curriculum and meet any demands made by the local authority, if the school is a maintained school. This still leaves choices to be made both about the place of the arts and other possible subjects in the curriculum of older students and about the way in which other aspects of curriculum, which are not a formal part of the National Curriculum, may be included.

It must also provide for some learning outside as well as within the National Curriculum. This is partly described in the National

Curriculum Council publication *The Whole Curriculum* (1990) which suggests that there are themes and dimensions which should run through National Curriculum work and be part of the total curriculum experienced by students. These include:

Having concern for equal opportunities

It is essential in the first place that the staff are concerned with providing equal opportunities for everyone in the school to develop his or her potential, regardless of gender, race, social class or disability. This is discussed in greater detail in the next chapter.

Preparing for life in a multicultural, multilingual world and for closer links with Europe

The need for the development of appropriate attitudes is evident when we consider the way the world is becoming closer. We can no longer live and act in national isolation. We are part of a world where what one nation does affects others. Students need to be made aware of the problems and achievements of other parts of the world. We also need to take seriously the study of languages and encourage all those students who have the interest and ability to do so to study languages so that they are able to take advantage of the opportunities now available to work in other parts of Europe if they wish.

Having economic and industrial understanding

Many schools have experimented with ways of providing for this. Probably the best learning takes place through work experience and the discussion which should surround it. It will also be a legitimate part of work in geography. *The Whole Curriculum* suggests that it should involve helping students make decisions about such things as how to organise their finances and making them aware of government economic policy and the impact of economic policy on the environment. It also suggests that students need to understand enterprise and wealth creation and develop entrepreneurial skills.

There is an increasing pressure to introduce a measure of vocational education into schools. Vocational education, well taught, can offer as much breadth as any other curriculum. TVEI went some way towards changing the image of vocational courses as something for the less able.

Preparing for adult life through careers education

This is now an accepted part of the curriculum for secondary schools and should involve consideration of the skills needed to obtain and retain work as well as being concerned with the nature of the work individual students might be seeking. *The Whole Curriculum* suggests that this should involve access to individual guidance, systematic careers programmes, direct experience of the world of work, up-to-date sources of information about educational, vocational, training and careers opportunities and opportunities to compile and review a record of personal achievement, and, in Key Stages 3 and 4, a personal development plan.

Preparing for adult life through education in citizenship

Preparation for adult life should involve such things as preparation for life in a democratic society, knowledge of the law, rights and duties in employment, knowledge of public services, ideas for leisure and appreciation of the fact that ours is a plural society.

Developing concern for personal health through health education

The Whole Curriculum suggests that this area should include work on the misuse of drugs, tobacco and alcohol; sex education, family life education, safety, health-related exercise, nutrition, personal hygiene, environmental and psychological aspects of health education. It would seem to be particularly important to include some work on preparation for parenthood. We know from research that the early years are of considerable importance for children's future development. Parents can make a great deal of difference to children's later development by the way they bring them up. Courses in parenthood for both sexes provide opportunities to raise standards of parenting and improve the possibilities for the next generation.

Environmental education

Education about the environment will naturally be part of work in geography, history and science. The school needs to have a positive view of what is involved in education about the environment.

This needs to include knowledge of the way environments are shaped by natural forces and then by man. It should also consider the vulnerability of environments and the need for planning to ensure that we do not continue to destroy our environment.

The NCC publication also speaks of:

Developing skills in the following areas

Communication   The National Curriculum lays a good deal of stress on communication skills and it is particularly important to develop oral communication. However, it should not be forgotten that much communication involves movement, and work in drama can be particularly helpful here. Technology also involves communication through drawings and diagrams.

Numeracy   Being numerate means having the ability to apply mathematical knowledge. Many students find that they can perform the necessary operations in class but are unable to translate them into useful material in other contexts. Teachers need to look for applications of mathematics in all aspects of curriculum and work with the mathematics department so that students gradually become truly numerate.

Study   This is an area which should be taken very seriously by schools. Students should become increasingly independent in study as they grow older and this means that all teachers need to consider the contribution they make to the development of study skills. This is not only a matter of skill in using books and recording but also skill in asking questions, observing, interviewing for information, sorting out findings and organising them into a coherent report. The school needs to define the skills which students should acquire and decide where they are going to be acquired and practised. It should not be forgotten that many primary schools do much to develop study skills and the secondary school should build on this foundation.

Problem solving   Problem solving is a set of skills which can be found in almost every area of curriculum, but particularly in technology and science. It involves defining the problem, setting objectives, reviewing the context and then generating ideas and considering them before deciding which to use. Finally it involves selecting a solution and evaluating the result.

Personal and social education Personal and social skills involve self-knowledge and the development of a positive self-image. The school has much to do with this. As many students as possible need to experience success but at the same time each individual needs to come to terms with his or her weaknesses and regard them as areas for further development. Failure needs to be seen as part of learning. Building self-confidence is partly a matter of matching learning to individual students and partly a matter of seeing that everyone can receive genuine praise for something.

Social learning involves developing social competence in dealing with social situations and developing acceptable social behaviour; the ability to work with others to an agreed end, sensitivity to others and the ability to imagine what it is like to be someone else – a skill which can be developed through the study of literature as well as in the way some misdemeanours are dealt with. Students also need the ability to make moral choices, thinking through situations and considering how others may feel. This may be part of the work with the form tutor and part of social and personal learning as well as part of the study of literature and religious education.

Information technology This should be part of the work in many subject areas and all students should become competent in its use, able to use word processing not merely as a means of producing good-looking work but as a way of developing a piece of writing. They also need to be able to use spread sheets and databases for a wide variety of purposes.

These aspects of education may be dealt with as elements in their own right but many of them can be dealt with within work on the National Curriculum. Figure 5.2 may be helpful in deciding where each dimension and theme should be undertaken.

Religious education remains part of the compulsory curriculum though not part of the National Curriculum. A religious education programme in non-church schools is set out in local Agreed Syllabuses. Ideally this course should give knowledge of religion so that students are in a position to make up their own minds about it

		English	Mathematics	Science	Technology	Languages	History	Geography	Phys. education	Art	Music	Relig. education	Separate subjects
Themes	Economic understanding												
	Careers guidance												
	Health education												
	Citizenship												
	Environmental education												
Dimensions	Equal opportunities												
	Multicultural education												
Skills	Communication												
	Numeracy												
	Study skills												
	Problem solving												
	Personal and social												
	Information technology												

Figure 5.2 Themes, dimensions and skills

while having an understanding of the way religion affects behaviour and thinking now and in the past.

A final area of curriculum which does not feature in the National Curriculum or in *The Whole Curriculum* but which emerges from each person's experience and is affected by schooling is the process of acquiring a framework of meaning for life and a value system. This may be part of the work in religious education but it is also affected by much else that happens in school. Literature may affect students' views of values. So may science and technology. The way students are treated certainly affects the way they see themselves and the values and attitudes they begin to adopt. The examples given by staff also affect this. Teachers need to think about this part of the inferential curriculum.

Ensure professional standards of performance

Research on leadership in schools suggests that effective headteachers take a strong interest in the actual learning of students and give leadership to the teaching and learning in the school. A headteacher needs to be confident that heads of department know how teachers work in the classroom and this means that they need the opportunity to spend time in classrooms on a regular basis. This will, in any case, be a necessary part of appraisal. The headteacher also needs to be seen to be interested in what is happening in classrooms by spending some time observing teaching. A headteacher and senior members of staff will affect standards of performance by what they choose to praise, the occasions they check staff for performance which is not considered to be adequate and by what they say in public about good practice. They also affect teaching by the extent that they create opportunities for discussing learning and teaching and by the kinds of topics chosen for discussion on in-service days. Making staff accountable for examination results also affects standards of performance. A headteacher must be concerned in the first instance with the actual standards of teaching and the extent to which students appear to be learning but he or she also needs to check simpler matters, such as punctuality and marking and the way teachers use their time in the classroom. Reviewing the exercise books of each group systematically can be a discipline for teachers to see that the students' work is marked up to date.

Maintain oversight of continuity

A child's learning from the nursery school to Year 13 needs
coherence. The child needs to engage in it as one continuous
experience and there is evidence that discontinuity slows progress.
It also wastes the time of both students and teacher. Repetition
generally blunts the edge of motivation and makes students lose
interest in what they are learning.

It is particularly important at the present time that there is good
continuity from school to school, since students will move through
the National Curriculum at different speeds and it will be necessary for the secondary school to know and carry on from the point
each child has reached in the primary school. This will require
secondary schools to plan work at a variety of levels.

Creating continuity in school

If we do not create continuity for them, children may create their
own, sometimes unsatisfactory, continuity. We need to help and
support children in the process of transition from one stage of
education to another. Continuity between schools requires:

1 *The sending and receiving schools understanding each other's work.*
Ideally all primary schools contributing to a secondary school
should be visited by the teacher responsible for the intake year in
the secondary school and also by subject teachers. This can be
difficult when a secondary school serves many primary schools and
only a few students come from each. There should be a number of
meetings about curriculum between primary and secondary
teachers. The National Curriculum makes this more profitable
since there is a common pattern of what is being done.

One way in which understanding might be developed is to
arrange a joint field study to include students from the final year
of a primary school and from the intake year of the secondary
school. In this context the specialist skills of the secondary school
teacher may be useful to the primary school and the primary
teacher's ability in arranging group work to follow up field study
may be useful for the secondary school.

2 *Appreciation of the differences between stages and how these seem to the
student.* It is very easy for secondary school teachers to be

unsympathetic to the problems of students making the transition from primary to secondary school. The more that secondary school teachers know about the work of the primary school, the better they are able to to help new students to adapt to the much larger world of the secondary school. A teacher who is aware of the differences between primary and secondary schools can help students to deal with the new demands upon them and identify for them the ways in which they are expected to behave, particularly those which are different from primary school. New students are usually very worried about doing things which will get them into trouble yet they can easily find themselves behaving in ways which would have been acceptable in their primary school, but which are not acceptable in the secondary school. For example, in most primary schools, it is normal for children to go and get whatever they need for their work without asking permission. This may not be the case in some secondary classes and this needs to be explained to students. There are many unwritten rules of this kind and intake year teachers need to give some thought to how students should be expected to get to know them. Discussion between primary and secondary teachers about expectations in terms of behaviour and social maturity can be useful here.

Most secondary schools now arrange visits to the secondary school by primary students to be shown round by older students and to undertake some work. Some also arrange visits to primary schools by intake year secondary students to talk about their experience and answer questions. Correspondence between these two groups may also be useful and final year primary students may usefully be given the opportunity to interview secondary school teachers with responsibility for continuity.

3 *Appreciation of the need for continuity by teachers and readiness to make the effort required.* Teachers need to be aware of the many ways in which students can experience discontinuity and be prepared to work to reduce this to the minimum. The move from primary to secondary school is not the only point at which there is the possibility of discontinuity. There can be discontinuity between years, especially if there is a change of teacher in any subject. In particular there can be discontinuity between Years 9 and 10 and between the main school and the sixth form. The National Curriculum has reduced the break after Year 8 but if some subjects are not to be continued it is important that the courses experienced in

the first three years are seen as self-contained and constitute complete courses in their own right.

For a number of students the break between the main school and the sixth form is substantial. This will be true whether the sixth form is part of the school or is in a separate college. Much more is expected by way of independent study at this level and students need to have been gradually increasing the extent to which they are expected to work independently.

The last break is that of leaving school for work or going on to further or higher education. Schools are now preparing young people much more thoroughly for the world of work than in the past. Ability to settle happily into further or higher education depends on the one hand on the degree of independence in learning a young person has achieved and on the other the social maturity and ability to live and work with others which has been developed in school. Social maturity will develop only if students are increasingly treated as mature people, even if they find it difficult to live up to this expectation. A recent programme based on a survey of young people by the BBC and *Readers' Digest*, found many young people complaining that they were not treated as adults at the end of their schooling and that this was the difference between work and school.

4 *The involvement of parents as partners in their children's education.* The involvement of parents will be dealt with in detail in Chapter 15. Here it is important to remember that continuity concerns not only students but also their parents. Parents too need to be introduced to the ways of the secondary school and the expectations the school has for the partnership of school and parent.

5 *Understanding the structure of curriculum and the contribution of each stage.* The National Curriculum makes it much more possible for all teachers to see the curriculum as a continuity from the start of schooling to the end of the compulsory period. Teachers at the secondary school stage need to be familiar with the stages which have gone before and the way in which the child's skill and knowledge are being built up. In particular it will be a task for the secondary school to take students on from the point in the National Curriculum that they have reached.

Continuity is related to progression and development. Progression may be evident in the work of the individual students and it is valuable for the staff of a department to discuss what is meant by progression in their subject. This is not an easy task, partly because in the past we have tended to think of content in terms of knowledge to be acquired, rather than as skills and concepts. The National Curriculum is largely stated in terms of skills and concepts but it is still necessary to consider what may be considered progression in any given area. Students do not acquire concepts in one go. They take steps towards acquiring them and consideration of those steps can be extremely helpful in dealing with the slower learners. It can be salutary to see the way in which special school teachers are breaking down statements of attainment into much smaller steps to enable slower students to work towards the final statement.

Development is concerned with the way in which increasing maturity enables students to undertake tasks requiring more abstract knowledge. In physical education and subjects requiring strength and dexterity, the physical development of students will be important Both mental development and physical development, while happening naturally, can be increased and hastened by the exercise of physical and mental functions, but these need to be matched to individuals as far as possible.

6 *Understanding the differences in teaching approach at each stage.* If there is to be real continuity between primary and secondary schools, there should be a real effort to dispel the myths which teachers at each stage hold about each other and for each sector to understand the teaching approaches which are common at the previous or the succeeding stage. This means that teachers should visit each other and observe teaching. This will not be easy to arrange, but with determination it can be done. It is also useful to provide opportunities for primary and secondary teachers to discuss teaching methods as seen by teachers and to ask students about how they see teaching methods in their primary and secondary schools as differing.

One useful way of creating this kind of understanding is to have brief exchanges of teachers and students. A secondary school teacher may spend a week or so in a primary school and the primary teacher a week in the secondary school. This needs a good deal of careful arrangement but is an excellent way of establishing understanding. A more developed way of doing this is to have a joint appointment of a teacher to work part-time in the secondary school and part-time in the primary school. This can be a valuable

piece of development for the teacher concerned and can overcome some of the primary school problems about specialist skills
but may be difficult to arrange in the context of LMS.

7 *Appropriate use of records.* Records should help to ensure
continuity. Teachers need encouragement to look at records of
previous stages. It may be helpful to have a database giving each
child's progress in the National Curriculum.

8 *A policy and a programme to ensure continuity.* The continuity
policy should include statements of the following:

- the overall philosophy of the school regarding continuity
- the expectations of teachers so far as links with the primary
  sector are concerned
- the expectations of teachers so far as the further and higher
  education sector is concerned
- the areas within the school where teachers need to be concerned about continuity
- the responsibilities of particular people for continuity
- the way continuity will be monitored and evaluated

The school will also need an annual programme of dealing with
continuity issues, such as visits to primary schools and colleges and
overall evaluation of continuity.

Evaluation of continuity

The task of management is to monitor what is happening by way of
continuity and to see that discontinuity is reduced as far as possible. This might be done by talking with groups of students at
different stages, especially at the beginning of the autumn term,
when they will be particularly aware of any problems of
discontinuity. This is also a time for asking them how far their
teachers appear to be building on what has gone before and how
far they are repeating work that they have already done. This will
be particularly important for the intake year.

Another useful piece of monitoring would be to compare a sample
of students' exercise books brought from the primary school with a
sample of the same students' books at the end of the first term,
looking for evidence of continuity and at whether the standards of
work are being maintained or improved or are declining.

Departments might also be asked for evidence that the courses they offer in the first three years and again in the last two years of compulsory schooling are complete in themselves. The National Curriculum does not preclude this and it is important to remember that for some students the course in art or music which ends at the end of Year 9 may be all that that student ever does in these subject areas.

Continuity may also be evaluated by talking to students who have left the school about how they are settling into their colleges and employment.

Maintain an overview and encourage coherence

It is the task of management to see that the curriculum adds up. The National Curriculum now ensures that there is vertical coherence, in providing a total curriculum for the years of compulsory schooling. There is also a need for lateral coherence. It would be possible to teach the National Curriculum effectively but have very little linkage between the various subjects.

It is not easy at the secondary stage of education to organise in such a way that all teachers see their subjects as part of the total curriculum, each offering something unique to the overall education of the students. Yet it is important that students see subjects as contributing to total experience, rather than as a number of discrete entities. Teachers need encouragement to think in overall curriculum terms and it would do much to ensure that there is wide-ranging discussion and consideration of the curriculum as a whole if the following were agreed policy:

1 Each teacher should have the opportunity and encouragement to take part in general curriculum discussion. This means arranging regular meetings for this purpose which are open to everyone and encourage participation.
2 Each department should be required to make a brief written statement about the part their specialism plays in the overall curriculum and to review this regularly. Every member of staff should have copies of the statements from all departments.
3 All departments and teachers should consider the contribution their specialism makes to the themes and dimensions of the curriculum.
4 All departments should be required to state where their work touches or overlaps or relates to that of other departments and

should be expected to come to some agreement about how these areas should be managed.

Requirements of this kind must, of course, be introduced carefully into schools where this kind of thinking is new. An invitation to state what is being done to develop study skills in each department might be a helpful way of starting general curriculum discussion, since this can start from what is already happening and everyone can see that it makes sense for teaching in one subject to reinforce teaching in another. Similarly, requests for statements about areas of overlap between subject areas may encourage general discussion and could also encourage teachers to look at programmes for subjects other than their own in the National Curriculum.

Such discussion should in due course lead to the idea that the curriculum, as each student experiences it, must be considered as more than a collection of subjects. If the nature of each subject is to be fully understood, there is a need for some learning which crosses subject boundaries so that the contribution of different subjects can be seen and appropriate ways of tackling problems or ideas can be selected. It is when students undertake field work in a topic, exploring both historical and geographical aspects, use the opportunity to write in a personal way of the experience and perhaps draw and paint as part of it and study it from the scientific point of view, that they begin to see what each of these studies offers to the understanding of the experience. Such studies also bring students and teachers together to think about learning and problem solving more broadly. Technology also offers very good opportunities for this kind of cross-curricular work which can meet attainment targets in several subjects at the same time.

There is also a case for greater involvement of form teachers and year group teams in the curriculum. Form teachers should be looking at what their students are learning as a whole and considering how this fits into their personal and social development. There is currently experimental work in Sweden where a group of teachers takes a group of students all the way through the secondary school, teaching them for nearly all of the curriculum. Countesthorpe and Quinton Kynaston are also exploring the use of mini-schools. This kind of organisation allows a good deal of freedom in the use of time and the teachers can get to know the students really well. The scheme has the disadvantage that the teachers get less from their own subject department, but some of those involved feel that this is offset by the greater involvement with students' learning. This is a very radical solution, but the idea that the year team should have an overall curriculum responsibility for students in the year can help to unify the academic and pastoral elements in the school and involve all teachers in curriculum discussions.

Schools today are coping with many problems which were less evident in the past. Although the National Curriculum has dictated a good deal of what is done in terms of teaching, this still leaves the school with the difficult task of teaching about controversial issues such as race, sex, the use of drugs, political issues and much else of this kind. Today's students are growing up in a society where these issues need to be considered and schools are in a difficult position on many of them, since it seems that whatever they do will displease someone. It is therefore particularly important for the headteacher and staff to be clear and in agreement with the governors and as far as possible with parents about what they believe they are doing in the controversial areas.

Adults in today's world not only need to give thought to where they stand on such matters as sexual behaviour, but they also need to have the ability to make judgements about new issues as they occur. Students in school learning about the important issues of our time are simultaneously forming their own frameworks of understanding of the world which will help to determine their values and their views about issues in the future. They are also learning strategies for making judgements which can be applied in new situations. Teaching and learning about controversial issues ought to take place in the realisation that this is what is happening. It means being careful to put all sides of problems and encouraging students to see from many different points of view. It means discussing with them all the ways in which prejudice prevents our seeing other viewpoints. It means attempting to give them factual information and helping them to form judgements. The ability to think through controversial issues thus becomes one of the most important aspects of learning.

At the same time the school needs to be concerned with attitudes. The way young people are treated in school, the extent to which there is genuine sexual equality, the attitudes to race and to gender shown by the staff, are important in shaping attitudes. The extent to which the oldest students are treated like adults and expected to behave in adult ways is also important. Staff discussion

about these issues and how to handle them thus becomes a necessary part of dealing with the inferential curriculum. There will
never be consensus among teachers about many of these issues,
but there should be understanding of how different people feel
and an attempt to put over a balanced view to students

Parents also need to be involved. They need to know what the
school is attempting and where possible their aid should be enlisted.

Chapter 6

Organising learning

The National Curriculum and the school's statement of aims are starting points for the process of education. The other starting point is the individual student. Each child comes to school with his or her own unique set of experiences, interests and abilities and these affect the child's ability to take from what the school has to offer. The difficult task of management and of the classroom teacher is to bring together the students and the curriculum in such a way that the students learn.

The process of learning is rooted in experience. The words of the teacher or the textbook mean as much or as little as the students can bring to their interpretation. The teacher's basic task is to discover and build on the experience which the students already have, provide new experiences, help them to focus on what is significant within them and to sort, classify and order what they encounter, so that they become able to generalise from their experiences and apply the learning in new situations. This will involve extending their use of language, since words are important in enabling us to identify what is significant and store it in our minds. Alongside this process there is also a need to acquire and practise skills.

Learning might be judged to be effective when a student is able to transfer it to a new situation, preferably one which is real rather than contrived for learning and testing. In fact it is only when the transfer can be made in a real situation that the student can genuinely be said to have learned. This view of learning presupposes a greater amount of first-hand experience than is common in many secondary school classrooms.

The management tasks of organisation are as follows:

1 Organise the school effectively for teaching and learning.
2 Ensure that there are equal opportunities for all students.
3 Deploy staff and other resources effectively.
4 Provide a timetable.

Organise the school effectively for teaching and learning

It is the task of management to organise so that there is optimum learning for students, by deploying people, time and space to the best advantage. This involves grouping students in various ways for learning, sometimes attempting to form homogeneous groups and sometimes deliberately forming mixed groups. There may also be opportunities for students to learn as individuals, using computer-based or other resource materials and this opportunity is likely to increase as more programmes are produced for this purpose. Management must plan the use of time to provide a programme over the school year which uses the skills of staff and the space and other resources available to the best advantage.

Grouping for learning

Hargreaves speaks of the importance of the social group as a basis for acquiring common morality. He believes that this development happens as a result of being part of a cohesive group and notes that past secondary schools kept students in their form group with teachers moving rather than students (Hargreaves 1982). The demands of specialist subjects have made this no longer a possibility because most subjects now require a lot of equipment and there are also many advantages in teachers having their own rooms. The result is that students are less part of the form group or tutor group than they were in the past and this needs to be borne in mind and every effort made to foster stable groups, especially at the early stages of secondary education. Later on students may begin to identify with the larger group of the year or the school.

Group learning involves the opportunity to work as a group as well as being organised as a group. Much adult activity involves working in groups and students need to learn the skills of leading, following, sharing and contributing to group goals. Hargreaves notes that individuals need to learn that it is sometimes necessary to abandon one's own interests in the interests of the group or because one's interests encroach upon or negate the rights of others. He stresses the need for schools to prepare young people to be part of several communities as adults by being part of different groups in school (Hargreaves 1982). They are part of various groups in any case because of the need to organise large numbers, but the point he is making is that schools need to be aware of the learning potential of this and to make use of it in a positive way. He also stresses the value of the cooperative project for this kind of learning.

Since there are fewer teachers than students in a school, decisions have to be made about how students will be grouped for learning. There are a number of choices available:

Form/tutor group/specialist group Most secondary schools work on the basis of specialist teaching for a good deal of the time, sometimes keeping a group of students together for most subjects and sometimes differentiating them according to ability.

There are advantages for students of average and below average ability in having a limited range of teachers to whom to adjust. It is also possible in this context for teachers to work collaboratively to reinforce the work that each does and to see that the curriculum has coherence for the particular group of students. This is particularly valuable at the beginning of secondary schooling when too great a variety of teachers can be confusing. As students grow older they become better able to cope with a variety of teachers. More able students often find the variety of teachers stimulating and usually have no difficulty in adjusting to different demands upon them. There is also the problem of curriculum coherence, however, and it needs to be someone's responsibility to see that what each student experiences is not too confusing. As we have seen, the form tutor is in a good position to do this.

Ability/mixed ability grouping How far students should be grouped by ability is a difficult question to resolve because the knowledge we have demonstrates advantages and disadvantages both for grouping by ability and for mixed ability grouping.

The HMI report *Mixed Ability Work in Comprehensive Schools*, found that mixed ability work was associated with good relationships between teachers and students and among the students themselves. Mixed ability teaching appeared to raise the level of achievement for the least able where their needs were understood, but students of well above average ability were frequently not catered for and whole class teaching was common, even where the range was wide (HMI 1978).

The report did not set against this the disadvantages of grouping by ability, but past studies suggest that where students are grouped by ability there are expectations for groups at different levels which affect their performance. In particular there is a tendency to underestimate the less able and a belief on the part of teachers that there is more movement between groups than is actually the case. This last tendency is important in national terms. We tend, as a nation, to do less well with our below average students than many other countries where the expectation is that anyone can achieve if he or she is prepared to work hard.

Mixed ability teaching requires a different approach on the part of teachers, which differentiates work within the class. This is difficult to do when a teacher sees many groups within a week. There are two possible approaches. One is to select tasks which can be achieved at a variety of different levels, so that some students can go further than others. The other is to provide separate tasks leading to the same learning, with some materials which give more explanation. Subject departments may profitably build collections of material which will meet the needs of students of different ability studying the same topic. A third approach is to provide out-of-class coaching for students who do not understand within the class, using older students or parents as helpers. This may meet the need of less able students but there is still a need to extend the more able, possibly by providing more difficult tasks related to the learning which others are doing.

There is a good deal to be said for mixed ability teaching in the first year or at least the first term. This provides a stable group for students finding their feet in the school and gives students a chance to show what they can do in a new setting. It is, however, important that staff are aware of, and provide for, students with serious learning difficulties right away and make provision also for the more able as soon as possible.

The assessment of the National Curriculum will create its own demands in terms of the level students have reached, making it necessary in a mixed ability group to cater for students who have reached different levels. This seems likely to lead to some grouping by ability at an early stage. The most usual way of dealing with the need for ability grouping is to provide setting or banding and setting. A school can be divided into bands of broadly equal ability and set within those bands, or into bands of differing ability, allowing for finer setting where teachers wish it.

Both mixed ability and ability grouping have advantages and disadvantages and teachers need to be aware of these and allow for them. It is particularly important not to under-estimate students at the two extremes of the ability range. We need to convey much higher expectations to both the less able and the more able.

Friendship grouping When students first come into the secondary school they find settling in easier if they are with friends or children they know from their primary schools or home areas. They should also be encouraged to widen friendships.

Single sex/mixed groups Single sex grouping has traditionally been on the assumption that girls and boys had different curriculum needs, stemming from their different roles in the adult world. This is no longer a tenable view. The National Curriculum makes it compulsory for both boys and girls to study across the curriculum with no difference according to gender.

A few schools have experimented with single sex groups for subjects such as mathematics and languages where the sexes tend to perform differently, in order to see whether this can make a difference. Physical education tends still to be in single sex groups to match the differences in development between boys and girls in adolescence, but some schools are working with mainly mixed groups at least for some aspects of physical education.

Grouping by age/mixed age groups Most secondary schools, whatever their pattern of grouping, tend to group their students by age, keeping students of the same year group together. Mortimore *et al.*, studying primary schools, found that teachers tended to be unaware of which children were the youngest in the group and tended to regard them as less able even though they were making normal progress for their age (Mortimore 1988). It may be a good idea at the secondary stage to look at the ages of students considered to be less able to see if this still obtains.

Group size A further point to consider is group size. To some extent this is governed by the number of students, the size of the spaces available and by the demands of different subjects. It is also important to consider the size of group which is desirable for different activities and how to organise to provide the right-sized group for at least some of the time.

A good deal of school work is individual, with each student working alone at tasks set by the teacher. A natural progression from this is to resource-based learning and here the numbers involved can be as many as the space available and the person supervising can manage.

The grouping which is least used, because of the difficulty in creating it, is the small group of about ten to twelve students, which is a very good size for teaching and discussion. Discussion is an important way of learning which tends to be under used in schools. In a class group, students can opt out of discussion but it is difficult to do this in a small group.

One way of providing opportunities for small group work is for teachers to work with a group of students using some form of team teaching. Team teaching at the secondary stage of education usually involves a group of teachers whose subject expertise can be seen to contribute to a common end. It may involve a key lesson given to a large group followed by individual and small group work, including resource-based work. If the key lesson or film or television programme is shown to a large group which is only part of the total group, the remaining teachers and students can work in small groups.

The use of time

Time is finite and although in prosperous times we can increase it in one sense by increasing the staff of the school or by teaching for more of the time, we cannot produce more time for the students except by pruning non-classroom aspects of the school day. Improvements generally have to come from a better use of existing time. This is particularly important now that the existence of directed time sets definite limits on what teachers can be asked to do, although many teachers are still prepared to give much more than is demanded.

Any study of the use of time needs to start by analysing what is already happening. This means analysing how people are using time and sampling what is happening in different areas of the school. The school day needs examining, looking at the length of the day, assembly time, form time, breaks and lunch time and the time spent in moving between classes.

We really need a more flexible approach to the school day than is now common. Where a community school develops, it becomes natural to have some classes that go on later than the normal school day. This could lead to different ideas about the way the staff of a secondary school and its students work and some teachers and even some older students might prefer to start later or earlier and go on later or earlier on some days.

There is a strong case for a longer school day for older students. Those who go directly into employment often find the working day long and tiring because they have been used to something much shorter, even though it is usually followed by a period of home-work. Part of the transition might be gradually to lengthen the day so that by Year 11 students have a similar length of day to that in most places of employment, using the additional time for private study so that homework time is consequently reduced. There are problems about arranging this, particularly where many students come in by school bus, but it can be done, especially where there is a community use of the school. City technology colleges are already running a longer school day and other schools may need to keep pace.

Assembly time has been built into the legal framework of educa-tion but assembly does not necessarily have to be an assembly of the whole school. This is impossible in some schools because there is no space which would take everyone at once. Many schools now feel that a change in the law which would allow flexibility about time and place and in particular limit the number of assemblies each week so that they could be properly prepared would be helpful to the cause of profitable assemblies and religious observa-tion as well as to the school more generally. A mixture of assembly on some days and form time on others seems to be a more satis-factory pattern for many purposes. There is also a case, where there is pressure on specialist accommodation, for having assem-blies for part of the school at a time, with other groups using hard-pressed accommodation.

The breaks in the school day should also be examined to see whether they are contributing to the optimum use of time. In particular there needs to be a check on whether time is being taken out of the learning period in order to prepare for the breaks. Is what is happening at break times making work more difficult afterwards? Is the fact of having the whole school breaking at the same time creating discipline problems with misbehaviour in corridors and cloakrooms? The organisation of break times should use as little as possible of the time of staff and students.

Another time-consuming activity is changing lessons. While there is much to be said for each department having its own suite of rooms, it nevertheless results in a lot of movement on the part of students. This is lessened if the period length chosen coincides with breaks in the day or if there are a number of double periods.

The most important place to consider the use of time is in the classroom. Each student's time is precious and classroom organisation which holds some students back while others catch up or merely occupies some while others learn, is inefficient. There is much to be learned from following one student or one group of students around the school for a day and seeing what the programme looks like from their angle.

Blocking subjects together in team teaching or blocking subjects with adjoining accommodation can provide a longer space of time for activities where continuity would be valuable, as well as reducing time spent in movement about the school. It may be that subjects are taught on a fortnightly basis or there is a different concentration in each half term in order to make such provision. Field study benefits from this kind of provision and many craft activities are more effective when they are given a continuous period of time.

Time can also be blocked for some subjects without necessarily invoking team teaching. If a department or a faculty is timetabled with the whole year or a half-year group, arrangements about which teacher is responsible for which group of students becomes something for the head of department or head of faculty to decide with his or her colleagues.

Some provision of blocked time can also be made after examinations are over. Another way of providing blocked time is to take an occasional day out of the timetable, perhaps once a term, to devote to activities which benefit from uninterrupted work.

There is also a tendency to assume that everything must be studied all the time. If we think in terms of modules within subjects, based on particular parts of the National Curriculum, students can study a limited number of modules for a period and then move on to others. This allows for more concentrated attention on some subjects or groups of subjects for a period and is a more effective way of using time. There is, of course, the problem that if some subjects are left for half a term, students may forget what they have learned. This may be offset by the more concentrated learning possible when time is blocked. It also says something about what is likely to remain in students' minds when schooling is over!

Students also need training in using time well. This means that there should be a gradual move towards more of the time being planned by students. In practice, the development of coursework as part of examinations has encouraged this, but it needs to be taught and learnt from the beginning of secondary education. Secondary schools also need to consider how much attention has been given to this at the primary stage. Some primary schools do a good deal to train children to plan their time and the secondary school can build on this.

The task of management in all this is partly that of evaluating how time is being used and of making people aware of the importance of good use of time.

The use of space and equipment

A school needs to ensure that space and other resources are being used to the best advantage. The use of space is part of the time-tabling process but there are some general issues:

Provision of suites of rooms for different departments Secondary education is strongly specialist and in this context it is undoubtedly to the advantage of teachers if all the rooms in which a particular subject is taught are close together. This enables a department to share thinking and materials and equipment. It makes it easy to share aids of various kinds and to provide materials for students which otherwise might have to be carried a long distance. Rooms normally used by a small number of teachers tend to be better cared for and there is more use of display and self-service organisation of materials.

On the other hand, if teachers stay in the same place, students' movement needs careful handling. Subject suites also encourage departments to be separate when there is a good deal to be said for bringing different aspects of the curriculum closer together. The development of faculties may help this but equally may simply enlarge the group which remains separate.

Housing groups of different sizes Most schools have comparatively few spaces designed for groups which are larger or smaller than the average form. This poses problems for the school which would like to explore team teaching and it also poses problems at the sixth form level where comparatively small groups may be obliged to use a lot of space because no smaller rooms are available. This is basically a timetabling problem but there may be a case for dividing some rooms.

Selecting, storing and maintaining equipment   A school needs systems for ensuring that adequate care is taken in selecting equipment and seeing that it gets optimum use. This means checking that departments have studied the market adequately when selecting large items of equipment or substantial amounts of new material, perhaps arranging for them to visit other schools or talk to teachers elsewhere with experience of using the material or equipment under consideration. Specialist advisers also ought to be able to give good advice on purchasing such material.

The way equipment is stored and the system for accessing it affects it use, since anything which is difficult to obtain or often needing repair is likely to remain unused. The school needs a good system for checking that equipment is in working order and appropriately maintained. Money spent on technicians with responsibility for looking after equipment may be money well spent, since they save the time of teachers and ensure that money spent on equipment is equally well spent. While much of this is the responsibility of individual departments, management must see that it happens.

Ensure that there are equal opportunities for all students

Every school needs to have a whole school policy on equal opportunities for all students. This is not only a matter of equal opportunities for girls and boys and students of different races, important as these issues are. Schools may also discriminate without realising it against students of working-class background, against students with handicaps and against students of different abilities – sometimes the most as well as the least able. Many local authorities have policies and documents about equal opportunities and offer schools a good deal of guidance on these issues. It is necessary to have a whole school policy, emanating from staff discussion in which everyone has been involved. The involvement of the headteacher and senior staff and their support of the policy will be crucial. It will also be important to make the policy clear to parents. The whole issue of equal opportunities needs to be looked at regularly with particular reference to the hidden curriculum. Staff, ancillary as well as teaching, need opportunities to talk about their own prejudices and attitudes if they are to support a whole school policy.

Work on equal opportunities applies not only to work in the classroom but to the way the school runs from day to day. It will be important to see that no aspect of school life poses problems for any particular students because of their race, gender, class, ability or disability. The school's task is to educate all students to take their place in a plural society and to try to produce people who value this pluralism and enjoy its richness.

It is perhaps worth remembering that people generally have fundamental attitudes towards people who are different from them. These attitudes tend to be at a subconscious level and influence behaviour without the person concerned being aware of it. Very often the attitudes people hold towards those who are different from themselves have little to do with their experience and much to do with the attitudes their parents hold and with attitudes absorbed from friends and acquaintances and from the media. These deep-seated attitudes are difficult to change and the most that schools can hope to do is to change conscious attitudes so that they help to govern behaviour.

Gender

The last decade has seen considerable changes in the position of women in society and much greater consciousness of the need for girls to be encouraged to aim for careers which were not previously open to them. However, according to Joanna Foster, in a lecture given to the National Association of Inspectors and Educational Advisers, there are still only 11 per cent of women in top jobs and women's earnings are only 74 per cent of men's. Girls still do more chores at home than boys and it should not be forgotten that children's earliest experience in most cases is of mother in the home. It is probably also the case that for many students the example given at home is still of mother dealing with domestic issues, even if she is also in employment. It is also somewhat ironic that legislation designed to give women equal opportunities should have resulted in some schools having an all-male senior management team which makes it difficult to give girls a model of women in top jobs. It is therefore not surprising that girls still see themselves in subsidiary roles aspiring to a more limited range of careers than those aspired to by boys.

It is therefore important for the school to do everything possible to raise the sights of girls, increase their aspirations and encourage broader choices of courses and careers. This is partly a matter of providing models in situations chosen for work experience and in people who come to talk about their work. It may also be a matter of attempting to change attitudes on the part of boys, since some of the attitudes of girls are conditioned by the way boys regard and treat them. It may be valuable to give both sexes the opportunity to talk about this in a single sex group, sometimes with mature teachers of their own sex and sometimes with mature teachers of the opposite sex so that views can be expressed freely and an attempt made to influence the way both sexes think about themselves and about the opposite sex. The way teachers deal with each other and the way they talk about each other may be influential as well. It is also useful to discuss these issues with parents.

There is a tendency to regard gender issues as something concerning girls in particular. Boys have their own problems in accepting their gender, particularly where the local idea of masculinity is *macho*. They may need to be given confidence that it is possible for boys to enjoy the arts, to be gentle, to show emotion and have some of the characteristics which tend to be regarded as feminine, as well as the more masculine characteristics.

Race

A school needs to consider both multicultural education and antiracist education. Multicultural education will stem naturally from some aspects of the National Curriculum and schools today should be concerned not only with the European dimension of education but with world dimensions for students who are growing up in a world where what happens far away affects what is happening close to us. The celebration of holidays and festivals from different cultures, study of countries from which students of other races come, literature from other cultures and much else may all contribute. Discussion of characteristics of Asian languages as compared with European languages may contribute interestingly to the study of language. Teachers should constantly be looking at the curriculum with the multicultural approach in mind. Schools need to celebrate the diversity of their students and teachers need to show that they value students of different cultures.

It is much more difficult to tackle the question of race more directly. There should be opportunities for discussing human rights issues, items in the news, racial stereotypes, issues such as anti-semitism and much else. Drama offers a particular opportunity for exploring the feelings of others. History and geography both have contributions to make in discussion of situations in which racism has been evident. There are also opportunities to tackle the issues of racism arising out of incidents where there has been conflict between students of different races. There is the possibility that discussion and work on racism may reinforce rather than counteract prejudice but this is no reason to ignore the problems that exist. There is a constant need to learn about the best way to live in a plural society.

Issues of race are particularly important in all-white schools where it is easy to assume that there is no problem. Children growing up in communities where they seldom meet people of other races have a particular need to consider the effects of racism and to have a multicultural dimension to their curriculum. Schools in such areas may profitably make links with schools which have a more mixed population. Schools in all areas might also make links with schools in third world countries.

Social class

It is very easy to under-estimate working-class students, particularly if their speech is strongly regional. Our low expectations for such students probably have something to do with our poor showing internationally at the lower end of the ability range. This is compounded by the fact that such students often have low expectations for themselves, partly the result of low teacher expectation and partly of parental expectation. There is a cycle of expectation whereby parents, because of their own experience, have written off school learning as something not worth having, and pass this view on to their children whom they consequently do not expect to do well at school. This is in contrast to some other cultures where a much wider range of parents expect success in school from their children.

The task of the school is to try to raise expectations so that such students break the cycle. This again is something which a headteacher can influence by not accepting low expectations from teachers but constantly encouraging both teachers and students to aim high. Praise for teachers who do well with students of working-class background is important. It is also valuable to get across to working-class parents that the school has high expectations of their children and hopes that many will stay on into the sixth form and get better jobs by having more education.

Ability

Discrimination by ability is closely related to discrimination by social class. There is a good deal of evidence from research that we under-estimate students of low ability. It is interesting to compare the achievements of students in special schools for students with moderate learning difficulties with those of students of low ability in secondary schools. The students in special schools often do better although those in the secondary schools may well be rather more able in some cases. The National Curriculum demands that we make the curriculum accessible to all students and this may mean developing steps towards attainment targets for some students rather than aiming at them directly.

There is also a danger that able students will be under-estimated because they have chosen the easy path and do just enough to get by. It is, for this reason, important to see that teachers are aware of those students known to have exceptional ability and vigilant for others who may not have been identified. In a sense equal opportunities for such students means giving them different and more demanding opportunities than those given to others.

Students with disabilities

It is all too easy to assume that a student with a serious physical handicap also has learning difficulties, particularly in cases where the handicap limits speech. A child may have good intelligence but have been unable to develop it because of deafness or a speech problem. He or she may therefore be unable to show the ability which is there. Students with serious physical disabilities may also have difficulties in writing and using tools which may lead to an under-estimation of their abilities. We also tend to treat students according to their appearance and a student who looks extremely young or is extremely small for his or her age is likely to be treated in a more childish way than others, both by teachers and students. Teachers need to be aware of this danger and try to avoid it.

The equal opportunities policy

A whole school policy on equal opportunities would include the following:

1 A statement about the attitudes expected from staff towards all students, together with some comment about the kinds of students to whom it may apply in particular.
2 Information about what teachers should actually do to support the equal opportunities policy.
3 Statements about specific responsibilities for seeing that the policy is implemented.
4 Statements about the resources available to support the equal opportunities policy.
5 Information about the way the implementation of the policy will be assessed.

Assessing the equal opportunities programme

It is not enough to have an equal opportunities policy. There must be regular assessment of how well it is working. The people best placed to make this assessment are the students, although there must also be assessment and discussion by the staff. Questionnaires to selected groups of students may reveal aspects which are not evident otherwise and these can be followed up by discussions with small groups of students and then with staff. Parents may also have something to say about this.

Deploy staff and other resources effectively

Most headteachers inherit a structure and cannot easily make wholesale changes, partly because people are in post and might not fit a different structure and partly because reorganisation is always costly. However, LMS gives greater freedom to head-teachers to change the staffing structure, even if it is through the negative route of needing to lose staff to meet the overall budget. Although this is unfortunate, it can sometimes create ways of starting to implement desirable change. In any case, a headteacher who is clear about the changes he or she wishes to make can gradually move to a new structure over a period of time as opportunities occur. The important thing is to be aware of the advantages and disadvantages of different structures and to make judgements about how they would work in the particular school, so that a possible future structure gradually becomes clear.

Handy suggests that there are four sets of activities in any organisation:

1 Steady-state: This 'implies all those activities which can be programmed in some way, are routine as opposed to non-routine.'
2 Innovative/developmental: 'All activities directed to changing things the organisation does or the way it does them.'
3 Breakdown/crisis: This is largely self-explanatory but includes the unexpected as well as disasters.
4 Policy/direction: 'The setting of priorities, the establishment of standards, the direction and allocation of resources, the initiation of action, these are activities which form a category of their own, although there is some overlap with other sets.'

(Handy 1976: 198–9)

Handy goes on to suggest that parts of an organisation will probably have some activities falling into each of these categories. However, there is a tendency for some groups of people to have more of one kind of activity than another and to become better at that kind of activity. He concludes from this that there is a case for differentiation of groups with some having more of a particular kind of activity than other kinds (ibid.).

In schools, as in most organisations, all staff have a good deal of work in the steady-state category. Policy and direction are the responsibility of management even in the most democratic of schools, although much decision making may be delegated and there may be many collaborative decisions. The breakdown, crisis, unexpected situation tends to become the responsibility of the more experienced people and often falls to those who happen to be available at the time the crisis occurs. Innovation and development can be anyone's task, however, and many headteachers find that their young and inexperienced staff have much to offer. This suggests that it may be possible to create a structure in which there is an attempt to separate innovation from steady-state activities, perhaps forming a volunteer group with some members known to have innovative potential invited to join to look at possible developments, leaving the tasks of the day-to-day running of the school to the official leaders of the school community.

Beare *et al.* suggest a number of much more radical changes in the school as we know it. They believe that it is possible to re-structure schools to involve mastery learning in which students learn 'through their own efforts in dialogue and cooperation with their peers and with each other in peer tutoring'; or they can belong to cross-age groups in which the older students help the younger ones. This ties in with what Beare calls the vertical curri-culum in which 'all subject areas [are] divided into developmental units placed on a vertical grid. The students work individually or in small groups and teachers act as counsellors. Students have different rates of progress (Beare *et al.* 1989).'

This does not seem to accord with much of the work on effective schools which finds that a mixture of individual, group and whole class work is the most effective way forward. On the other hand there is something to be learned from it. Many schools do not give enough thought to the possibility of students helping each other and plan-ning their work collaboratively in some areas of curriculum. It happens in practical subjects but not in the more academic, though this is changing. The idea of dividing the curriculum into develop-mental units is also one which the National Curriculum would make comparatively easy and would enable students who are slower or those who have missed work to catch up.

Beare *et al.* also have ideas about the structure of the school. Like Handy they suggest four domains: routine operational management; planning and developmental; professional; political (Beare *et al.* 1989).

Each of these requires a different form of behaviour. Some people will take part in several domains and will need to act differently in each. They suggest that it is in the operational domain that the sorts of structures we now have operate most effectively. The planning domain will require temporary structures using task forces and project teams, each with their own leaders. In this context the organisation could involve people who have abilities in this direction. This is very like the innovatory role which Handy identifies.

Beare then suggests that there should be a domain which is concerned with the delivery of a professional service to clients. He sees the 'professionals' – the teachers – cooperating to pool their ideas and skills to ensure that there is the best possible analysis, that collective wisdom is accumulated for the person receiving the service and the most competent operation carried out. While this in one sense is no different from the way schools normally operate, an emphasis on 'clients' might well produce rather a different feeling and approach, particularly in relation to parents, where legislation and government propaganda are combining to create a different relationship between school and the parents they serve.

The final domain is the political. Here the writers suggest that the headteacher in particular has an important role in dealing with the various interest groups outside the school. They stress the need to work with power coalitions and lobby groups and, in effect, to manage the political scene as it affects the school (Beare *et al.* 1989).

These four domains have implications for the structure a school adopts. Their suggestion is for a situation which allows project teams to be formed which cut across other structures and for much decision making to be collegial.

The staffing structure a headteacher eventually develops is a means of achieving various aspects of the tasks of management. These can be distributed in a variety of ways and the distribution of tasks must be reflected to some extent in the money available for salaries. The staffing structure is also part of the communication system, since a headteacher may use it both to inform and to consult. It is closely related to the way the school is divided into units for learning and pastoral care.

A basic question in today's schools is whether to have a faculty structure. The advantages are that departments can be encouraged to work together and make the curriculum more coherent. There is also an advantage in that the group of faculty heads is small enough to work together easily, whereas the heads of department meetings can be large and include some people who are the only teachers in their department. The solitary teacher has much to gain from the faculty structure. The faculty structure is also a useful way of breaking the school into manageable units. Against this, many heads of department are concerned that their subject will not get a fair representation by a faculty head who may have a different specialism and may not be able to represent all departments equally well. It also makes an extra bureaucratic layer.

Another basic question is whether to have a vertical or horizontal pastoral structure. Many secondary schools see themselves as a series of year groups which are to some extent self-contained. The pastoral system thus operates within the year group and this fits well with the academic programme. It also offers opportunities for students to take responsibility at every stage of the school. Others operate a system in which each tutor group has a cross-section of students from different year groups, sometimes bringing together students from all years and sometimes dividing the school into lower and upper with tutors taking a group through that phase. This offers more opportunities for older students to take responsibility and in the tutor group that contains more than one age group, the teacher can get to know the students better over a longer period and the younger students can learn from the older ones.

Determining a structure also means deciding on the responsibilities which go across the whole school. Some schools are moving away from having two or more deputies to a flatter structure in which there are several people undertaking whole school tasks, some of whom are not teachers. The following areas need to be overseen by someone at a senior level, although the work might in some cases be done by someone else:

- curriculum, including communication through heads of department or faculty, timetable, curriculum development, examinations, evaluation of the academic programme and teaching;
- pastoral care and discipline, including communication through heads of year or house heads, students' records, students with special needs, home/school relationships, discipline issues, evaluation of these aspects of school life;
- administration, including day-to-day routine tasks, supply cover, staff duties, the school office, the school environment, health and safety, public relations, evaluation in these area;
- school finances, records, care of non-teaching staff, evaluation in these areas;
- care of teaching staff including induction, care of newly qualified teachers, staff development programme, appraisal, arrangements for staff selection, staff records.

A different breakdown would be for each senior person to be responsible for a section of the school, taking on oversight of the responsibilities listed above for that part of the school. There would still need to be responsibilities for administration, finance and non-teaching staff which would probably be the responsibility of someone other than a teacher.

Another way of looking at the breakdown might be to take from the ideas described by Handy and Beare earlier in this chapter (see

p. 74 and p. 75). This might then produce one group of responsibilities for the everyday running of the school, another for forward planning and policy making, another for client services, that is, the teaching programme of the school, pastoral care and relationships with parents and another concerned with looking outwards involved with building the image of the school, all aspects of publicity, fund-raising, work experience and links with employers, careers education and so on.

The pattern chosen by a particular school depends a good deal on the people who happen to be in post and the previous history of the senior management team. There is much to be said for the members exchanging jobs from time to time to increase their experience and skills, although this needs care, because not everyone will be equally capable in all the posts and acquiring the necessary new skills could take time during which the school might suffer.

A task for the headteacher and governors is to decide a pay policy for the school which rewards staff in a way which reflects the aims and goals of the school and the particular values which it sets out to represent. The pay policy should be clear to everyone. There must be decisions about which are to be the best paid posts and this will reflect both the state of the market and the values of those making the decisions.

There is also increasing pressure to make pay reward good performance. Schools will vary in their views about this and may have difficulty in finding money to implement such a programme. A major problem is how good performance should be judged. A policy which is seen to be fair might involve defining different levels of pay for different levels of performance. For example, the highest level might be offered to those who are seen to be outstanding, a second level to those who work well consistently, a third level to those whose work is generally sound, with a lower level for those whose work is below average. Someone would have to make judgements about these levels which would be accepted by those concerned and this would be time consuming and difficult. If this kind of judgement is made as part of appraisal, it ceases to be an effective means of staff development. If it is made in some other way, it will take time to make valid judgements. This may, nevertheless, be a good way of retaining good staff and encouraging less good staff to seek employment elsewhere.

The collegiate school

There is now a good deal of evidence to suggest that effective schools are those where there is a common and accepted culture which is widely shared. Beare *et al.* note that the culture:

> begins to show in the way the school is run, its furnishings, its rewards and punishments, the way its members are organised and controlled, who has power and influence, which members are honoured, which behaviours are remarked upon. All these things create the climate in which children learn and which is powerfully pervasive in those learnings.
>
> (Beare *et al.* 1989)

These things are evident in all schools, but it is where the culture is a shared one that it becomes effective in influencing everyone who is part of the school.

The culture of a school depends upon the values held by the headteacher and staff. The school needs to develop a philosophy which is based upon shared values and which informs everything that happens. Beare and his colleagues describe this as: 'a statement of assumptions, values and beliefs about the nature and the purpose of schooling, of learning and teaching processes and processes which support learning and teaching' (Beare *et al.* 1989).

The philosophy starts with the headteacher and governors and its development must involve the staff and to some extent the parents and students. There should be many opportunities for people to talk about what they most value in education, often in the context of making decisions about some aspect of the work of the school. It should be possible to refer decisions back to a set of beliefs and values to see if they accord.

Part of the task of the headteacher is to weave together the values held by the various partners in the educational process and part of it is to try to establish a common vision. Vision stems in the first place from the vision of the headteacher. This vision is communicated by everything that the headteacher does, the way he or she dresses, arranges his or her room, speaks to people, writes, the comments he or she makes about the work and behaviour of teachers and students and the events he or she chooses to attend. It is also transmitted by the way a headteacher uses time and the issues he or she chooses to address.

There are two reasons why the development of the school culture is important. To be effective a school needs to be very clear where it is going and have agreement about overall direction, so that everything that happens contributes to the learning of the students. In the second place, it is becoming increasingly important for schools to develop a public image so that people outside the school know what it is trying to do. Everyone connected with the school is part of the public image and it is to the advantage of the school if the image is what the headteacher, staff and governors would wish it to be.

How is the school culture developed? In the first instance there is a need for a lot of discussion about values. One school, for example, started an in-service day by asking all the staff to identify the things they considered most important in the work of the school. This was discussed in groups and gradually led to the formulation of a statement of philosophy with which all staff could agree. The staff then went on to consider the implications of this philosophy for different aspects of their work. Such an exercise might profitably involve governors and a sample of parents and might well be discussed also with groups of students. The more widely such issues are discussed, the more hope there is of achieving wide acceptance of a philosophy. The philosophy must also be applied very frequently to decisions about many different issues.

Within the school the culture is gradually developed by the way issues are dealt with, the way people are treated, students are spoken to, misbehaviour is managed, teaching methods are developed. Ceremonies and rituals and methods of honouring those who do well are all part of this process. Uniforms and badges and a school logo and public image in correspondence all contribute to the idea that this is a special group of people.

Also part of the process of creating a common vision and culture is the extent to which all staff are involved in areas of decision making, particularly those which affect them closely, such as the school development plan. This is not easy with a large staff but there are various ways in which it can be undertaken. In the first instance there will be issues which need discussion by everyone. These may be the subject of an in-service day, with staff working in groups to express their views about the issue in question. The decisions, whether taken by vote of the whole staff or by the headteacher and senior management team, need to be seen to reflect the views expressed.

Some issues may be discussed through meetings of heads of department or faculty or heads of year or house who have responsibility for representing the views of their teams and must feed back to their teams the discussion which has taken place. Other issues may be discussed by working parties which involve teachers at all levels in the school and report to a more senior group, such as the head of faculty meeting. Here again, it will be important that the views of the working party are widely known and taken very seriously.

Provide a timetable

The curriculum philosophy of a school needs to be translated into arrangements for teaching and learning and this means providing a timetable. A great deal of the work of timetabling can now be undertaken by computer but the variables and the preliminary work are still the same as when timetables were made manually.

Timetabling involves manipulating the five variables of curriculum, students, teachers, space and time so that a programme emerges in which the resources of people, space and time are well used, lessons are appropriately distributed across the day and week and students and teachers each have a programme which is satisfactory.

Curriculum

The advent of the National Curriculum has reduced the degree of choice at the various stages of the secondary school and this makes the timetabler's task rather easier. There are still areas of choice, however, particularly in the last two years of compulsory schooling. There may also be a need to consider how the work of the most and least able is to be differentiated.

Students

Decisions have to be made about groupings of students for learning. Relevant variables for timetabling are the numbers of students in each year, groupings which cannot be timetabled simultaneously and the groups in which students will learn. With younger students the teacher contact time is usually 100 per cent but as they grow older there is a case for reducing the contact time so that students learn to work independently. Sixth form students are normally expected to have private study time but if this is to work well, work on study skills and independent learning needs to start earlier.

Teachers

The timetabler needs information about the numbers of teachers, their skills and competences and decisions about the groups they teach. A preliminary for timetabling is to decide on the amount of time that each teacher will be in contact with students. The level of contact time affects group sizes.

There is also a need to consider priorities in the use of teachers. Some schools feel it is very important for the intake year to get a good start and groups at this stage are therefore made as small as possible. Other schools prefer to put resources into later stages and the sixth form in particular may make inroads into staffing.

Space

The timetabler needs to have information about the numbers of rooms and their capacities and specialist functions.

Time

Decisions are needed about period length and the pattern of the day or week. There are advantages when most of the lesson changes are at breaks in the day, although this can result in too long a period for some subjects. Many schools prefer to have the bulk of their work before lunch and have a shorter afternoon. It may be possible to have a flexible lunch hour in which teachers and students have a break according to the way they are timetabled.

There should also be some consideration of other activities to be fitted into the timetable. It may be possible to timetable some meetings. Form time is important if there is to be a learning programme related to it.

Timetable blocking

Timetable blocking provides a number of opportunities. It involves timetabling together a group of teachers and a group of classes, so that they have some flexibility of time and grouping. Blocking can be for a single subject. This devolves responsibility to the head of department and enables the staff concerned to group students as they wish and re-group if necessary for particular purposes. It allows for team teaching or for large groups to see a film or television programme together.

Alternatively there can be mixed subject blocking, where a group of subjects which may or may not be related are timetabled together. This could be used for more integrated work in the first three years.

Chapter 7

The management of change

Politically motivated change is accompanied by greater commitment of leaders, the power of new ideas and additional resources; but it also produces overload, unrealistic time-lines, uncoordinated demands, simplistic solutions, misdirected effort, inconsistencies, and under-estimation of what it takes to bring about reform.

(Fullan and Steigelbauer 1990)

This statement will strike a chord in the minds of most headteachers and teachers in today's world. We have never experienced so many external demands for change from without in such a short period of time and this has placed enormous pressure on everyone in the education system. Headteachers are in the position of having to manage large changes as well as changes they and their staffs may wish to introduce. The management tasks are as follows:

1 Manage change effectively.
2 Manage decision making effectively.
3 Plan effectively.

Manage change effectively

Most people are ambivalent about change. They want a certain variety in their lives so that every day is not the same as the last and so that there are differences which make life interesting. At the same time they may not welcome the kind of radical change which makes substantial new demands, making life more difficult or threatening them in some way.

The teaching profession has shown itself to be highly adaptable and flexible in managing the changes which have been demanded in the last few years. The fact that this has not been properly appreciated makes it no less of an achievement. The difficulty is that the changes are likely to continue, since we are, in a sense, living through a kind of revolution in many aspects of our lives. If changes are likely to continue the task of headteachers and senior staff in managing them is crucial. Headteachers must constantly be looking outwards from their schools, trying to anticipate where demands will come from next as well as looking to the changes needed to meet the goals of the school. The management of change is an important part of the role of the headteacher.

What do we mean by change? It includes positive ideas such as innovation, development, progression, renewal, reform and so on and negative ideas like disaster and catastrophe. Change is not necessarily good or bad in its own right. Change can be planned or unintentional. It can be voluntary or imposed, threatening or non-threatening. However it comes, people have to make it their own if it is to be effective. Change of any kind usually requires attitude changes on the part of those involved and it is this that creates some of the difficulty.

Fullan and Steigelbauer point out that change is not something which can be done *to* others. They must become involved in the change and attach personal meaning to it so that they make it their own (Fullan and Steigelbauer 1991). People also interpret demands for change in terms of their previous experience and what they know. They see change as good if it accords with their particular values. Many of the changes being thrust upon schools at the present time represent values which are foreign to teachers and this is the cause of some difficulty.

Change from without may come with its own inexorable time-table and managing this kind of change is a matter of planning so that people have time and opportunity to express their feelings and doubts before getting down to working out with them how the change can be implemented. It is important to involve people in the planning and working out of detail so that they gradually make the change their own.

In the case of change from within there is great skill in choosing the time to make a change. When a headteacher comes new to a school, some changes are expected and by talking with people he or she can gauge which changes would be acceptable at that time. As time goes on there needs to be preparation for changes. This involves a good deal of discussing possibilities, perhaps looking first at aspects of the school's work which many people see as a problem. It is very often possible to use an agreed problem in order to effect change in other desirable directions. For example, work on how to cope with students with special needs may lead to a consideration of how students generally are taught and the need to make a variety of provision within the class, so that students of all abilities have something which challenges them. Work on improved record keeping may lead to consideration of the need to discuss individual records with students and help them to set goals for themselves. A lot of successful change in schools is a matter of looking for a way in which change can be seen to meet people's expressed needs.

Change planning has both a formal and an informal side. Once a change has been agreed by staff there will be a need for a long-term plan which brings in the change over a period. Alongside this a headteacher may have a personal programme for change which depends upon using opportunities as they arise. A teacher may come with a suggestion to try something which the headteacher sees as a desirable change and he or she may encourage the teacher in the hope that others may be interested and want to change in similar ways. A parent may make a complaint which involves the headteacher in talking to a teacher or group of teachers and perhaps suggesting a different way of doing things to meet the problem which the parent has posed. A good headteacher or head of department asks questions of staff which may lead to the kind of changes he or she sees as desirable.

The ability to assimilate change is much dependent upon the school climate and culture. It will be easier in a school where teachers are used to working together, are open with each other, see failure as a means of learning rather than something to be ashamed of and share each other's problems.

Where a headteacher and staff have long-term ideas about major changes they will need a change structure which incorporates both planned and informal change. Complex changes may need to be broken down into a network of smaller, interdependent changes where movement is made when the situation seems right. Sometimes, for example, the departure of a key member of staff provides the opportunity for change. Sometimes an event which is otherwise unwelcome provides an excuse for change – for example, the need to make cuts may force a school to change its ways of working in some areas. These may not always be undesirable changes.

Ideally a school may aim at change by consensus where all the staff feel that they can work together to change in ways that they agree are desirable. The larger the school, the less likely it is that consensus will be achieved, but within sections of larger schools, such as year groups or faculties or departments, it may be achieved and this can build up the impetus for change across the whole school. This will not happen quickly. A group of people needs to work together for quite a time before they begin to think together and develop a momentum for change.

A different approach to change, where appropriate, may be to explore a new way of working with a small group of interested teachers and to implement their ideas as a possible spearhead for wider development. In this context it is very important that the experiment succeeds, because others will be watching and if it fails will be less willing than before to try anything new. A negative experience of change makes future change more difficult.

An important aspect of managing change is that of giving support to teachers as the change takes place. There is often a low point after about half a term when nothing seems to be going right and this is the point at which the senior management needs to be about the school encouraging people to continue and assuring them that things will gradually work out. It is also important to give recognition and reassurance to teachers. This is always important but particularly so when teachers are involved in changing ways of working. Change can be damaging to confidence and teachers need reassurance that what they are doing is leading to success. It may also be necessary to exert pressure to continue with the changes during the period when they seem to be going badly.

Change eventually needs to become embedded in the system. The existence of the school development plan supports this. Each change will require a budget and eventually a policy as well as a timetable and the need to plan and budget annually for school development means that changes can be planned and possible changes weighed up against one another.

The following points may be valuable in considering change:

1 There is likely to be continuing demand for change from external sources. It is therefore important to develop a culture in school which accepts change as a normal way of life.
2 Change is most likely to be successful when people see a need for it.

3 It is most likely to be successful if those involved in implementing the change have been involved in planning for it.

4 Change involves uncertainty and can be threatening to the self-image. Those involved therefore need a great deal of support, reassurance and help during the process of changing.

5 Individuals have to make sense of change for themselves before it becomes part of their way of working. This may need a good deal of discussion.

6 Change frequently involves conflict and disagreement. This is part of the process of individuals making sense of change.

7 Successful small-scale change is a useful way into larger change.

8 Obstacles to change must be recognised and taken account of in planning change.

9 People tend to misinterpret and misunderstand anything which seems to threaten them.

10 Change is a slow process. It may take several years for a change to be fully accepted and implemented.

So far we have been considering change from the point of view of the teaching staff of the school. However, the school is concerned with various other groups of people. Governors will need to be involved in plans for change processes from the beginning. It may also be a good idea to include some governors in some of the staff discussion about change so that they have a clear idea of how teachers feel about it.

Another important group of people who will be affected by change are the students. There should be plans to discuss change with them, particularly the older ones. Students tend to be conservative about changes and may feel unhappy for a period with changes which affect them. Some of this unhappiness can be avoided if they are involved in some of the discussion about planned changes. Fullan and Steigelbauer, writing of the involvement of students in the process of change, ask, 'What would happen if we treated the student as someone whose view mattered in the introduction and implementation of reform in schools?' (Fullan and Steigelbauer 1991).

Parents are also concerned when schools change and ways of involving and informing them are very important. The parent governors will be involved in discussion through their membership of the governing body and it may be a good idea to involve them in some staff discussion so that the parent view is represented.

There may also be situations where it is politic to involve non-teaching staff. The caretaker and clerical staff, in particular, may be affected by a decision and may need to be consulted before it is implemented or in some cases involved in the discussion.

Change may also involve the use of outside consultants, who may be members of the local advisory service or other people whose services are bought in to help with the change process. The use of a consultant, particularly one who is seen to cost the school money, is often helpful in convincing people first, that the need for change is serious and second, that they need to act on the recommendations of the consultant. This may also result from inspection, particularly where there is pressure to follow up the inspection with an action plan.

Manage decision making effectively

Decision making is an essential part of the process of change and has many ramifications. Current demands for democratic processes lead to an expectation of open government where many major decisions are made by the group rather than the individual.

A leader has not only to get decisions made but implemented. A decision is most likely to be properly implemented when those involved in the implementation feel commitment to it. People are most likely to feel committed to a decision that they have been involved in making.

There is also another reason why others besides the head-teacher should be involved in decision making. There is a limit to what one person's mind can hold by way of alternatives. Where decisions are made by an individual the choices available will be more limited than when decisions are made by a group. There is also greater possibility of error or of missing some important issues which will affect the implementation of the decision.

Decisions might be categorised as follows:

1 *Immediate decisions.* Some decisions have to be taken immediately. No one calls a meeting to decide that the school should be emptied because part of it is on fire. Decisions about changes in timetable or cover for absent teachers may have to be made quickly by one person in order that the school may work. Whilst problems may arise because people make foolish decisions under pressure, most of the immediate decisions made are accepted by others without too much difficulty.

2 *Functional decisions.* Decisions in this category may be made by one individual or a group which has delegated responsibility for particular functions. Such decisions are normally made within a pattern which is known and understood and, while there may be occasional objections, there is rarely passionate opposition if it is accepted that the people or groups making the decision are within their rights in making it. Even in this situation those concerned would be wise to do a certain amount of negotiating and sounding out opinion before coming to a conclusion. For example, it is normally accepted that the headteacher and governors will make decisions about the staffing structure of the school; the head of department may be expected to make decisions about which teachers teach which groups. In both these cases there will be a need for consultation and negotiation.

3 *Strategic decisions.* Strategic decisions are those which change the overall arrangements about how things are done, often affecting many people. Decisions of this kind need a great deal of discussion and a measure of consensus if they are to be acceptable and successful. They must carry people with them if they are to work properly. A unilateral decision by the headteacher of a secondary school to introduce mixed ability teaching will be disastrous if the teachers are not prepared to carry the decision through and change their teaching style to meet the changed circumstances.

Each of these kinds of decision may require a rather different treatment and much skill is involved in deciding which decisions are strategic and need to be widely discussed and perhaps decided by majority agreement. Even before discussion starts the wise headteacher will sound out some people whose views might be representative so that the topic is introduced taking known views into account.

The way staff view how decisions should be made depends a good deal on the history of the school and how decisions have been treated in the past. A staff which has become accustomed to very little consultation may come to see almost all decisions as functional and are often disinclined to become involved in time-consuming decision making and resentful at being asked to do what they feel the headteacher and senior staff are paid to do. Conversely a staff which has been used to being consulted on most issues will be resentful if decisions are made without consultation, even if these could reasonably be seen as functional.

A school which operates largely on functional decision making, with individuals at different levels making decisions without a great deal of consultation, may well be efficient, providing that those who are making the decisions are competent. Decisions will be made on more limited evidence and thinking than would be the case where more decisions were discussed and this will be a loss, but there will be fewer meetings than in more democratic institutions. In a static situation this might very well be acceptable to those involved if there is also a high level of autonomy in the classroom.

The staff of a school where many decisions are seen as strategic will spend a great deal of time talking, both formally and informally, about the best way of doing things. This will contribute to their development both in their current posts and in preparation for later managerial posts. They are also likely to have a higher level of commitment and job satisfaction. On the other hand it must be accepted that recent changes have placed enormous pressures on teachers, leaving less time for more general discussion and group decision making. The choice of which decisions to make collectively is very important. The leader's task is to get the best mixture of functional and strategic decision making, taking into account his or her own style, and the views of his colleagues and the community.

Drucker suggests that there are four criteria for determining the best solution to a problem: the risks associated with each course of action, which alternative gives the greatest results with the least expenditure of effort, the timing and the people involved (Drucker 1968).

The last two of these are extremely important. Each school staff is different and decisions about change which are accepted happily in one school are unacceptable in another or require a great deal of talking and thinking through. Timing is also crucial for change and the decision making process leading up to it. It is possible to make a change unacceptable by introducing it at the wrong time, when people are deeply involved in something else, for example. There is great skill in choosing appropriate timing and it can best be judged by talking to key individuals. Sometimes a change will need to be broken down into a series of smaller steps which people are prepared to take.

The following general points may be made:

1 The best decisions are often those taken as near their implementation as possible. This is the thinking behind Local

Management of Schools (LMS). While broad decisions may be taken at the top, other decisions should, where possible, be delegated to the level of the action.

2 The development of agreed policies may lead to an increase in the number of functional decisions. The right to make decisions because of the function one holds requires trust on the part of colleagues. Leaders at all levels in the school must be seen to have integrity. It is also important to get the right balance between functional and strategic decisions. This is likely to vary from one school to another.

3 An organisation needs to accept the view that once a decision is made, by whatever method, those in management roles must implement it as well as they possibly can, whatever their views as individuals. It is easier to foster this view where consultation procedures are good.

4 Considerable dissatisfaction is generated when people think they are making a decision and then find that they are simply being consulted and that the decision is actually being made elsewhere. There are three ways in which people can be included in decision making as part of the process of change:

   (a) They can be *involved*. Involving people in a project implies allowing them to make the final decision. This will commit them to the decision, but a headteacher has to be fairly sure that he or she will be happy with what they decide because credibility is lost where people get the impression that they are making a decision which is later vetoed. The best way to avoid this is for the headteacher to spell out the parameters within which the decision is to be made, making clear the kinds of decision which would not be acceptable.

   (b) They can be *consulted*. Alternatively, people can be consulted, but in a context where it is clearly understood that the headteacher or the senior management team will make the final decision, taking the views expressed into account. This is less motivating and those advising the headteacher will be less committed to the decision but it may be the best way forward in some circumstances.

   (c) They can be *informed*. Whatever is decided, there will almost certainly be some people who simply need to be informed about what is to happen. These may include students and their parents, non-teaching staff, the LEA and in some situations, the governors, depending upon the nature of the particular decision.

When delegating to a group it is important to consider its composition. A group in which the majority has negative feelings may work badly and it may be a good idea to create *ad hoc* groups for some things, particularly if the normal decision making groups contain a high proportion of people who are apathetic or antagonistic to change. An *ad hoc* group may gather together people who will contribute positively, perhaps with a small number who are rather more negative. It is often possible to influence people with negative views if they are part of a group which thinks positively.

Headteachers who use this approach have to be careful to carry their normal decision making groups with them in such a plan. It may be possible to organise so that the more senior group delegates ask the *ad hoc* group to report back, or the *ad hoc* group may be regarded as experimental with the brief of trying out ideas with a small number of people before they are considered more widely.

Where there is no real option about the composition of the decision making group, it is important to consider its brief very carefully and present it in terms which its members find acceptable. A traditionally minded group, for example, might be prepared to look at the school's procedures for assessing students' work and progress, but not be prepared to look at the process of evaluation more widely. In the process of looking at the lesser aspect the broader questions may arise and interest in them be generated, so that people become ready to discuss them.

Plan effectively

Some aspects of planning have already been discussed in Chapter 3, on the school development plan (pp. 24–33). The analysis of areas for change given in that chapter should help to identify systematically the areas in which change is needed. It can also be helpful to analyse the situation in order to assess what the problems of change might be. A useful starting point is to consider the necessary pre-conditions for the innovation being planned. There are a number of basic pre-conditions common to many kinds of innovation and others which may be relevant to the particular school and to the ideas being considered. The analysis in Figure 7.1 presents these items so that the reader can assess how far he or she has suitable conditions for a particular development. The first column should be completed by inserting a lettered grade to represent the importance of this aspect for the particular innovation. The five columns on the other side are to assess the situation in the school, so far as the particular project is concerned, against each of the pre-conditions. For example, in making a change in the organisation of the school day which would give better use of the facilities of the school, the motivation of the staff might be seen as fairly important and graded B in the first column. However, the actual motivation for this change might be at a comparatively low level and given a minus grading. Experience and ability will probably not be relevant for this kind of change and would be graded D or E but attitudes may be important. If high grades in the first column go with low grades in many of the other columns this could mean that it would be wise to go fairly slowly and perhaps undertake the change in small steps rather than all at once. The two grades together give a picture of how difficult a particular change may be.

The motivation of those involved in most changes is important. Where the people likely to be most closely involved are not motivated at all towards the change in question it may be wiser to consider a less drastic change as a step towards the eventual goal.

Many changes need people with appropriate experience. This may mean sending people to visit other places or finding ways in which they can hear about comparable experience. One must be realistic about the skills and knowledge of the people involved while at the same time having high expectations.

Any change requires certain attitudes initially on the part of those to be involved. They have to be ready to consider change, flexible enough to cope with it and to some extent open-minded. However, it is not possible to deal with attitudes in isolation. It is often best to work at the nuts and bolts of making a change, looking at it as changes in tasks to be done. Changes in attitudes may then follow.

The attitudes of students also need to be considered. There may be work to do in convincing students of the need for change. Good ideas can also founder on parental and community opposition, so it is worth thinking about this at the early stages, taking into account the attitudes of parents and community, including the school governors.

Successful change requires trust between the various groups of people involved. Teachers must trust each other if they are to work

Grade	Pre-condition	++	+	av	–	– –
	Motivation of those involved					
	Experience of those involved					
	Ability/skill of those involved					
	Knowledge of those involved					
	Attitudes of teachers					
	Attitudes of students					
	Attitudes of parents/community					
	Relationships: teacher/teacher					
	Relationships: teachers/head/senior staff					
	Relationships: teachers/students					
	Relationships: school/parents/community					
	Resources: space					
	Resources: time					
	Resources: materials/equipment					
	Other pre-conditions					

Figure 7.1 Pre-conditions of change

together and it may take time to develop the kind of trust which allows change to be successful.

Change needs time – something which our politicians do not appear to understand. It may be necessary to convince people that the change under consideration will enable them to work more effectively but will require an investment of time to get started.

Change may also depend upon having the necessary resources. This is one of the more difficult aspects of change at the present time. People may need convincing that some change is possible without substantial expenditure on new materials or that the necessary expenditure can be met in some way. Budgeting for change is an important part of planning.

The time needed for discussion and preliminary consultation and its value should not be under-estimated. A headteacher needs not only to consult but also to be seen to be consulting widely. It is therefore wise, particularly for a headteacher new in post, to be systematic about consulting, noting people who have been asked to give opinions and making sure that those in key positions have been consulted. It can be useful to make a list of who should be involved in a major decision, who should be consulted and who should be informed. This enables the headteacher to be reasonably sure that no one is being left out. Leaving people out is a sure recipe for opposition. Preliminary consultation may also give people the opportunity to volunteer to take part if the change is of the kind where this is relevant. This can be valuable in starting an innovation, since volunteers tend to be more motivated.

Detailed planning can then begin. Some suggestions for planning have already been put forward in Chapter 3 (see pp. 24–33). One useful way of planning is to use network analysis, which was described in Chapter 3.

Headteachers and senior members of staff have a number of strategies at their disposal for getting people to work with them. The following points may be considered:

1 People are more prepared to consider change in areas where they see a problem. Problems are a good starting point. They always exist but need seeking out and clarifying since often they are not what they are immediately perceived to be.

2 It may be useful to ask people what they would like to change and if possible start with some of the suggestions they make. People who do not want change tend to suggest things which

are not within the school's jurisdiction or make suggestions
which are only half serious. The right climate is important in
making this strategy work.

3 A leader can create situations which bring people up against the
need for change. Asking someone to study a particular problem
in the school or to teach a group which exemplifies the problems which need to be tackled may make them more ready to
consider change.

4 People may be attracted by opportunities which bring out the
benefits of change. For example, a plan for teachers to visit
other schools to see particular work in action and report back
to the staff may be helpful.

5 Working groups can be created in which those who are likely to
influence others are placed with those who might benefit from
that influence. Where this is done, it is necessary to have more
people who will be a positive influence than those likely to be
negative – otherwise the influence may work in the wrong
direction.

6 People who have something to offer to the planned changes
may be invited to pioneer some of the work.

7 Situations can be created in which people want to be seen to do
well. For example, a small group of people might be invited to
research something connected with a desirable change for the
staff and be given time to undertake this and be given the
opportunity to report publicly.

8 It may be possible to offer someone time to undertake some work
for a change. The period after examinations is a good time for this
kind of work, although it may be worth considering the possibility
of substituting for a teacher for a week as would be done if the
teacher were away ill. The fact that this is costing a good deal may
be an incentive to the person concerned to deliver at the end of
the period. On a longer-term basis it is possible to plan so that
there is time for development work within the timetable.

People set about finding solutions to a problem in several ways.
They may simply hold the problem in mind for a time and encourage others to do the same in the hope that someone will produce
a possible answer. This often works and constant practice in producing solutions seems to improve the ability to generate further
ideas, especially if people are in the habit of absorbing ideas which
might be useful sometime. The staff of a secondary school usually

includes a large number of people who are fluent in ideas if one can find the best way to tap this source.

One can work more positively than this, however, perhaps visiting schools which have tried different ideas, reading round the subject and talking to people within and outside the school who may have something to offer.

There are also some strategies which are useful in this context. For example, a group can try brainstorming a particular topic. This involves seeing how many ideas can be generated, recording them all, working as fast as possible and not worrying about whether they are viable or not at this stage. It is sometimes helpful to set out to generate a given number of ideas before going further.

Alternatively, sheets of paper, as many as there are group members, each headed with a problem or part of a problem, are circulated and each member adds an idea as the sheet comes to him or her. If this is done using OHP transparencies, the ideas suggested can be discussed, leading eventually to a decision about which should be pursued further.

The point of these strategies is that they involve everyone in having the ideas which are needed to take the plans a stage further. It also gets people away from being negative and helps them to become involved.

Eventually the stage is reached for deciding on a solution to the problem in hand. Where one of the strategies outlined above has been used, it may be helpful to make a preliminary selection of ideas and then to make a table of pros, cons and points to note about each idea. Individuals can do this from their own point of view and then from the point of view of other individuals or groups.

It gradually becomes possible to select the final ideas to be used. It may be that, in the end, parts of different ideas are chosen and a composite solution is created. The important thing is to be sure that there is enough discussion and consideration of different ideas before a solution is reached.

Finally, the solution is put into practice. The following points need to be borne in mind:

1 It is wise not to try too much at once. If relevant and possible, a pilot scheme should be tried before too many people are committed to major change. It is usually best to carry this out with people who are committed and enthusiastic and who are likely to demonstrate that the change works.

2 All the people involved in the change should know what they
are doing and there should be insistence on adequate preparation and thorough checking when everything is ready to go.
Mistakes are costly in goodwill, particularly if some colleagues
are ambivalent about what is happening.

3 Checks are needed either with someone observing what is
happening or with those concerned being asked to report at
given intervals so that the progress can be monitored.

4 People involved in change need a lot of encouragement from the
headteacher and senior staff who should praise everything that can
be praised and be ready to talk over problems and difficulties and
maintain morale if things seem to be going wrong.

The final stage of dealing with innovation is to evaluate what has
happened. It is only when there is thorough evaluation that people
learn from any activity. The evaluation should be planned at the
same time as the activity so that it becomes an integral part of what
is happening and so that evidence for evaluation can be collected
as the project goes forward. It should involve the following:

- Set dates for reviewing what is happening and looking at a
  number of aspects of the change.
- Identify particular matters which need to be investigated. The
  following questions might serve as a check list:
  • What are the outcomes of this work?
  • Are there any unexpected outcomes?
  • What are the advantages of what has been done?
  • What are the disadvantages?
  • How have the students/teachers benefited?
  • What do students/teachers feel about the change?
  • Could there be any further improvement?
- Consider the evidence available and the particular kinds of
  evaluation which are possible. If this is considered in advance it
  is often possible to find evidence which is available without very
  much additional effort.
- Decide on the type of evaluation. Details of different types of
  evaluation are given in Chapter 16 (see pp. 225–9).
- Decide who will be responsible for evaluation. The people responsible should, if possible, be neutral about the innovation.
  Failing that, an evaluator with strong views needs to be balanced
  with an evaluator holding opposing views. The status of the
  evaluator will also make a difference. The headteacher or deputy

will get different information from that offered to a more junior teacher asking the same questions. There are some advantages in having an evaluator from outside the school if possible.

There are a number of reasons why change is difficult. Wilson suggests three areas of difficulty:

1 Fear of change in the way things are done and the impact of this on customary ways of working. There may be concern from parents if a school starts to work in unfamiliar ways. Teachers too may find unfamiliar ways of working worrying because they are uncertain about the outcomes of what they are doing. Students are often the most resistant of all to change.
2 Fear of loss of job or career prospects. The fear of redundancy is at present very real. There is also the fear that change may limit promotion prospects by reducing possible promotion posts.
3 Fear of loss of power, prestige or status. This is a very real fear in times when schools are being reorganised to cope with falling rolls. It can also be a fear if the organisation of the school changes.

It is especially difficult to get people to look objectively at the need for change when the school is in difficulties. There is often a tendency for people to want to discuss those aspects of the problem which are the responsibility of others and to avoid discussion of those elements where something can actually be done. Or they may put all their energies into defending the *status quo* and leave none for making the necessary changes. In this situation it may be necessary to allow a certain amount of ritual blaming of others and exploration of non-solutions before people will be ready to work at solutions that are within their own power. A leader may need to bring people back again and again to what is possible and be firm in insisting that a programme is worked out and adhered to. In the current climate it may be essential to see that changes occur quickly and without the kind of caution recommended in much of this chapter.

Problems can occur in any context because of status difficulties. Status makes it difficult for some people to admit that they could be mistaken or that the way they have been doing things for years might be improved. Something may go wrong and no one likes to mention it because of the seniority of the person most closely concerned. A programme of change may fail because the teachers involved in organising it are too junior in status or service for others to be prepared to accept their role. These are problems which only the most senior staff in the school can deal with.

Chapter 8

Marketing the school

It is now clear that schools are in competition for students and that they therefore need to take marketing the school seriously. Schools are in the business of public relations.

Oxley defines public relations as 'the management of all the relationships that exist between a complexity called an organisation and all the individuals or other groups with which it interacts' (Oxley 1987). Planning for good public relations involves identifying the groups with which the school interacts and finding out their characteristics.

Public relations cannot now be left to chance. The school that relies on its previous good reputation to ensure that students keep coming may gradually be outdone by other schools where there is a greater awareness of the need to sell themselves to the parents. This will, of course, vary with the position of the school. A school which is the only one in an area is obviously in a less competitive situation than one in an area where several secondary schools compete for students. Nevertheless the school with little competition still needs to carry its parents with it. Money spent on the right kind of public relations will be well spent if it brings more students into the school, together with their budget allowances.

Schools will need to use the following strategies:

1 Survey the views of students, parents and community.
2 Analyse strengths, weaknesses, opportunities, threats.
3 Set objectives for public relations.
4 Organise the marketing of the school.

Survey the views of students, parents and community

One of the major problems about marketing schools is that people have different values. Teachers have their own several values and, in a good school, individual values come together to create a school philosophy and school values which may not be those of the community the school serves. In any case the community will consist of different groups, each of which has its own values. The school therefore has to be aware of the values of those it serves, while at the same time remaining true to its own values and making these clear to those who are considering sending their children there. A school which submerges its own values to meet those of the groups it serves may end up pleasing no one. One of the things it is marketing is its values.

Good public relations involves identifying the characteristics of the various groups the school serves and this will be necessary in order to set realistic and detailed objectives. In the first place this will be a matter of studying the local environment and the range of students for whom the school is the nearest secondary school. It may then be a matter of going further afield and identifying further groups whom it would be valuable to attract. It may also be a matter of finding out what the opposition is offering.

Governors should be an important factor in the school's public relations work. The governing body represents the local community and should be able to reflect for the headteacher and staff some of the views held locally. It is therefore important that governors share the overall philosophy of the headteacher and staff and this demands a partnership between them.

Studying the local environment in terms of the kinds of parents the school is serving may best be done by sampling the views of parents. It would be unrealistic to ask for views from all parents because of the time involved in analysing this kind of survey. It is therefore a good idea from many points of view to make it clear to parents that different groups will be asked for views from time to time so that, over the period their children are in the school, most parents are likely to be asked for their views. Where the clientele is largely middle class, it will be comparatively easy to get views on different aspects of the school from parents by sending them a questionnaire. Where it is not, and particularly where there are numbers of parents who do not speak English, it may be a good idea to involve students in helping to compile and get replies from their parents to questionnaires which sample parental views about schools and what they consider to be important in education. It will also be valuable to get students' views on similar questions, since they too are clients of the school.

A study by Elliott *et al.* suggests that many parents value the human qualities of schools and the happiness of their children at school above examination results although they see these as important. They found that parents 'associated happiness with the child's personal and social development at school, their increasing capacity to communicate with others and thereby create satisfying personal and social relationships' (Elliott *et al.* 1981) This view tended to be more widely shared by middle-class than working-class parents. They wanted schools to balance academic provision against social and personal development. If this is so then students' views about the school will be particularly important.

Yorke and Bakewell studied factors of choice in a group of five secondary schools which represented, on the one hand, parents from modern family housing in the higher income groups and, on the other, parents from less affluent council estates. They found that the three factors of overall importance to all groups were location, past examination results and help available for students with special educational needs. For the first group of parents the sixth form was important, but not for the second group. The first group also thought past examination successes very important whereas the other group thought they were only 'quite important'. The first group thought the number of students in the school quite important but the second group was not concerned about this. A larger number of the second group thought that provision for special needs was very important (Yorke and Bakewell 1991).

Forster describes a study at Newcastle University in which 60 per cent of 72 students interviewed said that they chose their secondary school (Forster 1991). This suggests that it may be important in marketing the school to give particular attention to potential students in their primary schools.

There is also a case for regarding the public as more than parents. Employers are an important group for secondary schools and the views of neighbours of the school, local shopkeepers, estate agents and other people in the locality all help to create a public view of the school, which is often based on ignorance. In finding out about various different groups, these people should not be forgotten. A number of schools have surveyed the views of employers about school leavers and students on work experience and have also sampled their views of what they want from young people and what they think school should be about. It may be helpful to invite other local people who are not parents, to school events so that they have some idea of what the school can do.

Analyse strengths, weaknesses, opportunities, threats

Cave and Demick suggest that the whole group of people whose views need to be consulted should be regarded as stakeholders, a group which should be taken into account in marketing the school. They suggest that the school might ask itself the following questions:

– How clearly have we identified our stakeholders?
– In what ways can the various stakeholders influence or make demands on us?
– How thoroughly are the needs of our stakeholders identified?
– How can the needs/wants of the various stakeholders be identified?
– How can the needs/wants of the various stakeholders be reconciled?
– What priorities do we establish in relation to these?
– How effectively do we manage key stakeholders?

(Cave and Demick 1990)

They go on to suggest the 'SWOT' analysis in relation to stake-holders – an analysis of the schools' strengths, weaknesses, opportunities and threats. This is not the same kind of analysis as a school may make for its own benefit, but one which lists strengths, weaknesses, etc. in relation to parents in particular and then other stakeholders. Thus the geographical situation of the school may be a strength if it is situated in the middle of its possible catchment area and on major bus routes, but a weakness if it is a long walk from the nearest public transport.

Set objectives for public relations

Fletcher, describing the results of a competition on marketing schools, stresses the need for detailed objectives and quotes a school where one objective was to attract 'articulate and middle-class parents who would traditionally have chosen schools further afield in the public sector' (Fletcher 1991). Another gave 'parents who do not speak English, many of whom are illiterate' (ibid.). In general the competition found schools poor at stating marketing objectives. The first task is therefore to set clear and detailed objectives. Oxley suggests that the first objective is for the organisation to be known and understood (Oxley 1987). This is undoubtedly an important objective for schools who need to be proactive in making the school known to the public.

Organise the marketing of the school

The picture a school creates in the mind of the public depends upon a number of factors. Some of these are the result of a direct attempt to influence the views of the school held by the various stakeholders. They include all the ways in which schools have attempted to sell themselves in the past – school events, newsletters, press articles, contributions to local radio and so on. In future there will also be the publication of examination results, truancy rates and four-yearly inspection reports. Although the way in which these are presented will be dictated, there is nothing to stop a school providing a commentary on each of them, showing in particular the progress which has been made year by year, or, in the case of examination results, giving information about the stage the first year were at in the National Curriculum on entry to the school and the value added in terms of examination results.

Fletcher noted that 'it is important to get the whole school committed – teachers, ancillary staff, students, parents, governors, everybody involved in the school. If you have mixed feelings and mixed ideas you are going to get bad publicity from the people who actually work there' (Fletcher 1991).

Behind the direct methods are all the indirect methods which are often very important in forming opinion. The following might be noted:

1 The way people are received in the school is of paramount importance. A welcoming attitude both on the telephone and in meeting people may make a great deal of difference to the way people subsequently view other aspects of the school. They can easily be put off at the beginning. A visitor needs to be able to find the way in easily and see immediately where the reception is. Some schools use senior students as receptionists and this is a very valuable experience for them as well as being a

good advertisement for the school, provided that the students are trained and can spare the time to do this. In any case the school secretaries have a very important role here. The time someone is kept waiting and the readiness to make and keep appointments is also important.

2 The impression a school makes does not stop at reception. At the time of transfer from primary school individual parents will be visiting a number of secondary schools and comparing them. Time and personnel need to be allocated to this task, which must be well organised. Meetings for prospective parents also need to be well organised and it can be helpful to arrange that some part of the meeting is in small groups with a teacher answering questions in each group. It can be tempting to lecture too much to prospective parents on the grounds that there is so much to tell them. It may be better to leave more time for them to ask questions and find out what they really want to know. Tours of the school might be undertaken with senior students so that parents can talk to young people who are actually experiencing what the school can offer. Here again this is useful experience for the students but they need some training in doing this job, so that they show off the school and themselves to the best advantage.

3 The appearance of the school is an important selling point. The entrance hall is particularly important. It needs to be attractive, with comfortable seating for anyone who is waiting and perhaps examples of students' work as well as plants and flowers. The outside of the school is also part of the impression the school makes and needs well-kept grounds and as little litter as possible. Students need to be constantly made aware of the way in which the appearance of their school matters.

4 The appearance of students coming to and from school is seen by the neighbourhood, which will draw its own conclusions. The appearance of students requires constant vigilance on the part of staff.

5 Written communications of all kinds carry more than the obvious messages. The school needs a logo and its own style in the layout of communications. It is now so easy to provide high quality written communication with desk-top publishing that no school has an excuse for poorly laid-out or badly duplicated material. It is also worth noting what makes people attend to written messages or ignore them. People will attend to messages that are:

(a) written to them personally;

(b) clearly of use to them;

(c) in language that they can easily understand. It is worthwhile being aware of what is jargon in the eyes of those not involved in education as well as trying to put messages into fairly short sentences, with important points highlighted in some way. At the same time the message should not be patronising;

(d) well laid out so that what is important is easily seen. Plenty of space in laying out type helps to make the message more obvious;

(e) in tune with their own views and values.

6 The extent to which parents are consulted about their views and the way in which this is done and is seen to be done may make all the difference to them feeling that they are genuine partners in the education of their children.

Public relations needs someone for whom it is a major responsibility. This should be someone fairly senior in the school, particularly good at making relationships, perhaps working with a small committee. The tasks of that person include the following:

- surveying the views of the stakeholders at intervals so that public relations work is properly informed;

- working with colleagues to identify the school's strengths, weaknesses, opportunities and threats so far as public relations are concerned;

- working with colleagues to develop and implement an action plan for public relations;

- making all members of the school, teachers, students, ancillary staff, aware of their responsibilities for the picture of the school which is developed by parents and by people locally;

- making contact with people who provide possible avenues for showing what the school is doing, for example, local press and radio stations;

- evaluating public relations projects.

The action plan needs to include a description of all the activities which are part of the plan, the phasing and scheduling of these activities, their cost and the way in which they will be evaluated.

Chapter 9

School administration

In the literature of many countries, the word administration is synonymous with management. In Britain we tend to see administration as the backup to management; the tasks that need to be done for management to function effectively, and it is in this sense that the word is used here.

The management tasks are as follows:

1 Oversee the administrative work of the school.
2 Control the school finances.
3 Be responsible for the building and environment.
4 Ensure conformity with health and safety legislation.

Oversee the administrative work of the school

Every school has a number of tasks to do which are not part of the teaching process yet which require the knowledge and expertise of a teacher. These include such matters as some of the work on examinations, some pastoral care issues, different forms of assessment and many others.

The following is a list of some of the many tasks which need to be undertaken by a member of staff. Of each task it might be asked:

- Does this task require someone at senior level?
- Is it a task which must be undertaken by someone with teaching skill and knowledge or could it be done by the secretaries or the bursar?
- Could it be shared with a more junior member of staff as a development opportunity for him or her?
- Is it being done as efficiently and effectively as possible? Would a greater use of micro-technology make it easier to do?

Major administrative tasks	Persons responsible
Preparation of school prospectus	
Preparation of school handbook/materials for students	
The induction and allocation to classes/tutor groups of intake year	
Arrangements for subject choice	
Subject choices for examinations	
Administration of examinations	
Administration of SATs	
The preparation of the timetable for the next year	
The process of students applying for places in further or higher education	
Careers guidance, work experience and the placing of students in employment	
Pastoral care	
Maintenance of student records	
Arrangements for reporting to parents	
Arrangements for students at break and lunch time	
Lunch provision	
Public relations	
Maintenance and care of building and grounds	

Figure 9.1 Administrative tasks

Staffing and the recruitment of teachers	
Staff development	
Arrangements for support of newly qualified teachers	
Arrangements for induction of new teachers	
Arrangements for cover for staff absence	
Arrangements for staff appraisal	
Preparation and updating of staff handbook	
Care of the staffroom	
Care of non-teaching staff	
Parental involvement	
Industrial links	
School finances	
Public relations	
Health and safety	
Other responsibilities	

Figure 9.1 (Continued)

The task of the headteacher and senior management is to see that the work is distributed equitably and undertaken efficiently. When the list in Figure 9.1 has been completed, with names against each task, it is possible to consider whether the work is fairly distributed, whether more people could contribute, how satisfactory the arrangements for each item seem and whether information technology could improve efficiency.

The school office

Every school requires non-teaching support for the administrative and clerical tasks required of it. These have increased considerably with LMS. Some of the tasks are part of the accountability structure of the LEA or DFE; others, such as examination entries, are external requirements. There are also tasks concerned with the governors, parents and the community.

Within the school there are clerical tasks related to the day-to-day life of the school, to the curriculum, to individual teachers and students and to personnel issues. There is also now a considerable area of work for the governing body and in relation to school finance.

The appointment of a school bursar provides a senior member of staff who might be expected to deal with the management of the school office, although its effective working is still the responsibility of the headteacher. The more a headteacher knows of the work of the office, the more effectively he or she can use the support it offers.

Clerical work in school may be broadly classified under the following headings:

- the collection, organisation, maintenance, storage, retrieval, provision and communication of information
- staff records, salaries, time and other personnel matters
- accounting and management of the school finances
- the processing of orders
- the provision of curriculum materials
- correspondence and telephone
- enquiries and reception
- examination work
- inventories
- sales
- school meals
- filing

Any consideration of the effectiveness of the way work is done must start from an assessment of the actual task. One way of doing this is to ask those concerned, as part of an exercise involving them in seeing if any of the pressures of work can be relieved, to keep a diary for a few days detailing how they are using their time. This may need to be tactfully introduced so that it is not seen as a preliminary to cutting staff. A good starting point is to ask people to write down how they are spending their time for just one day, then look with them at what they have written and try to make broad headings under which further analysis could be carried out. The list should then be checked to see if it includes all the normal categories of work, classifying it in order to find the answers to questions such as the following:

– How do the office staff use their time and skills?
– Is the work sensibly distributed?
– Are there areas of work in which there is difficulty in meeting deadlines?
– Are there times when the pressure is exceptionally high?
– How many interruptions does each person get? How far is this a problem?

The answers to these questions will give some information about the effectiveness of the use of time by the office staff. The people concerned need to be involved in looking at this information and deciding whether it warrants any change in the way things are done.

The use of information technology in administration

Information technology is increasingly used to deal with the administrative tasks of the school. Its great advantage is that information can be reformed to serve a variety of needs. Desk-top publishing is enabling schools to produce materials for many purposes which look attractive and give a good image.

The CIPFA publication on the local management of schools suggests the following objectives for information technology:

– reduce the time required to provide letters, reports and documents by using word processing;
– offer a single database of student information capable of producing information in a range of standard formats responding to specific search requests;

- produce standard statistical reports requested by the local authority or the DFS;
- provide the means of analysing, controlling and auditing all financial transactions;
- aid the school timetabling process and extract statistical information from the timetable;
- offer a single database of staff details with the capability of extracting essential information as required.

(CIPFA 1988)

Other management information which might be held on computer includes:

- staff information
- supply teachers
- class contact time
- attendance rates
- student names and addresses
- information about parents (for example, with whom the school should communicate and telephone numbers in case of student illness)
- students analysed by age and their curriculum options
- groupings of students
- examination entries and results
- National Curriculum assessments
- destinations of students
- careers service data
- equipment and materials purchased and held
- consumable supplies used including such things as energy
- services provided (for example, those of maintenance operations)
- selected performance indicators

A further consideration is that of security. School hardware needs to be marked so that it can be traced and recovered if stolen. There is also the matter of security of data. Staff and parents and older students need to be convinced that information about them held on computer is available only to certain people. They should be made aware that they are entitled to access to any information about themselves or their children held on the school computer. This suggests that access to the computer that holds the majority of school information should be via passwords. It will also be important to make and keep backup discs for all the standard information and in view of the possibility of fire in the school, they should be kept in a fire-proof safe. Databases take a long time to build up and their loss creates a considerable problem.

Control the school finances

One of the biggest changes that has happened in education over recent years is local management of schools. This has given schools much more freedom in managing their affairs and opened the door to better ways of managing the money available. At the same time it has posed considerable problems for headteachers and governors for many of whom much of the work of managing finance on this scale is new.

It is interesting to note that the movement to give schools this kind of freedom is happening in other parts of the world as well as in Britain. New Zealand, Holland and parts of Canada, Australia and America have all developed schemes giving schools greater independence. It remains to be seen whether this move will result in higher standards of achievement. It should result in better spending, since those nearest the action should be in a better position to make decisions about spending than those further away.

Delegation within the school

The principle that spending is most effective when it is near the action, implies that there should be considerable delegation within the school with individuals responsible for the budget for their area of responsibility. Each department or faculty thus becomes a cost centre with its own budget and responsibility for spending. This means that not only the headteacher but also heads of department or faculty must become knowledgeable about accounting. It also means that there must be clear systems for dealing with the budget which cover the way the money is allocated, the way that accounts are kept and the way spending is monitored. These systems will not only be needed by the headteacher and the school bursar but by all members of staff who have budget responsibility. Within departments and faculties there should also be discussion about the budget spending so that all members of staff are aware of and have a say in this at some level.

Caldwell and Spinks suggest that budgeting should be set in the context of collaborative management in which policies are worked out for every area of school life and are the responsibility of a policy group, which would probably be the governing body (Caldwell and Spinks 1988). Each area then develops a programme for work which must be seen to conform to the various policies, not only for that area of work but to policies generally. The programmes are then costed and put in priority order and are presented in an agreed structure on no more than two sheets of A4 paper.

Caldwell and Spinks also suggest that the plans and costing for each area of work in the school should show how they relate to the school and departmental policies and that the broad planning and costing should be outlined according to an agreed structure so that all can be gathered together in a booklet which everyone can see. They suggest that this structure should include statements about the nature of the programme, its aims or purpose, a statement of broad guidelines, a plan for its implementation, a list of the resources required, a plan for evaluation and a list of the team which has been involved in drawing it up, together with a note of the school policies which it meets. Their suggestions include the idea that the programme should be written out on a form so that all the programmes have a similar format. and that proposals should be given priority labels 1, 2 or 3. Programmes should not only include the academic work of the school, but issues such as pastoral care and care and maintenance of the building and grounds (ibid.).

They go on to suggest that there should be a 'reconciliation' group whose task it is to reconcile all the programmes with the overall budget. This would be a group of senior staff who would use the priority ratings from each department to decide how best to reduce the programmes to a level possible within the overall budget, where this was necessary. The programmes would then be revised in the light of this and would eventually go to the policy group who would check that they met all the policies.

Budget responsibility allows the school to ask questions about the cost of educating students. It is possible to know how much is being spent on each student and on each subject and this leads to questions about whether money is being spent in the most effective ways for achieving the aims of the school.

Strain suggests that there are two ways of looking at budgeting. Incremental budgeting means taking last year's budget and modifying it appropriately to meet this year's targets. This gives stability and limits the debate but may neglect problems. Alternatively a school can use zero budgeting which involves reconsidering spending each year with budget holders justifying their claims. This means justifying the budget request in terms of existing and new activities and giving a valuation of the benefits accruing from each of these activities (Strain 1990).

Most schools will probably use a modified version which incorporates some aspects of both incremental and zero budgeting, asking each department to decide their priorities with the costs of each individual activity. Priorities above a cut-off line decided by management are continued and those below rejected. It is also possible to consider the implications of discontinuing existing activities. It is important that budgets reflect realistically the work that is planned. This may require a good deal of discussion and negotiation. If they do not reflect planned work, the budget holders will not feel committed to achieving their targets.

In drawing up departmental or faculty budgets it will be helpful if items are allocated to particular heads of budget agreed by the school as a whole. Rolph lists the following categories of expenditure:

- salaries
- energy costs
- rates (local taxation)
- equipment (education) purchases
- resources materials – library, etc. (education)
- examination fees
- equipment (maintenance and administration)
- materials (maintenance and administration)
- services (educational, maintenance, insurance)
- rental cost of equipment
- staff training and travel

He also categorises planned expenditure into four levels:

- mandatory
- essential
- useful
- it would be nice if we had one of those

(Rolph 1990)

Mandatory costs are those which are a legal responsibility. Essential costs are those which are inescapable but not a legal obligation.

Salaries

The major element in the budget is salaries, which are about 67 per cent of the total budget. The *LMS initiative: local management in schools* notes that schools may be concerned with the following categories of staff:

- full-time teachers
- part-time teachers
- supply teachers
- welfare assistants
- administrative and clerical staff
- nursery nurses
- technicians, resource assistants and librarians
- caretakers and cleaners
- mid-day supervisors
- school meals and grounds maintenance staff'

(CIPFA 1988)

Each of these categories of staff has its own salary pattern including the time at which salary increments become operational and its own conditions of service. Headteachers need to have some familiarity with all of these.

The same paper notes that schools need to compile a list of appropriate salaries and associated costs for each category of employee. The following points may be noted:

1 Schools will need to calculate allowances for employers' national insurance and superannuation. National insurance varies according to whether individuals have contracted out of the state pension scheme.
2 Pay awards must be allowed for in annual budgeting and this includes national insurance and superannuation. Superannuation will be proportionate to the pay award.
3 Schools are now free to decide on the number and levels of allowances within the rules laid down by the Pay and Conditions document. There should be a policy on this which is reviewed regularly.
4 Vacancies and staff turnover may lead to savings or to higher expenditure. It is not wise to reckon on savings from vacancies.
5 Overtime is difficult to estimate. It is easiest to build on last year's figures, but it should be monitored carefully.

6 Schools need to make an assessment of their possible need for supply cover for both planned and unplanned absence. It is important to consider how absence for INSET can be dealt with. It may be possible to timetable so that supply cover is not always needed. Some members of staff may also need cover for public duty as magistrates or councillors or for trade union activities or jury service. Some of these costs are recoverable. A number of LEAs are considering arranging insurance for cover for long term absence. The school can also arrange its own insurance and would be wise to do so if it is grant maintained.

7 It will be necessary in many places to budget for advice and consultancy where these are needed. This may be a matter of budgeting for specific advice on certain aspects of work, such as the design and furnishing of a laboratory or for an advisory teacher to work with the staff of a particular department; or there may be the need and the opportunity to budget for more general advice on an agreed regular basis. This may come from LEA sources or from higher education or professional consultants or from industry. It may also be necessary to budget for peripatetic teachers for special needs or for instrumental music. In some cases it may be necessary to include the cost of superannuation and national insurance in the fees charged but in other cases these will be paid by the person's main employer.

8 Some schools may wish to share staff with other schools so that the teachers concerned can be fully employed and minority interests catered for. In this case superannuation and national insurance will be *pro rata*.

If departments or faculties are seen as cost centres, their budgeting must include calculations about the amount of staff time that they will need for the various groups of students. These can be left as units of time, to be reconciled over the school as a whole or, alternatively, the school can decide to include staff salaries in the programme budgets. If these are not included, the major part of the expenditure will not be recognised. On the other hand, staff are likely to be reluctant to allow salary information to be made public. One way to overcome this problem is for departments to work on the average salaries for different types of staff (teaching and ancillary) for the whole school, calculating this as the cost of a unit of teacher or technician time. This enables realistic budgets to be constructed and helps people to see the real cost of educating students. It also makes for a more balanced comparison of the costs of different areas of curriculum.

Income

The main source of money for LEA schools will be through the formula funding but there are other sources of money which might be considered. Rolph lists the following:

- income from lettings
- school fund and student-derived income
- home–school association/PTA funds
- covenanting schemes
- services to the community and local industry, for example, reprographics, equipment hire, consultancy
- industrial sponsorship or subsidy
- bequests from former students

(Rolph 1990)

In addition, charges may be made to students for individual music tuition, education and transport outside school hours and the cost of board and lodging on residential trips, subject to remission in the case of hardship. The school may fix these charges.

A school is free to decide its policy over lettings. A charge must be established which covers caretaking, cleaning, heating and lighting. It will also be necessary to state what facilities will be available for the fee; kitchens, for example.

Monitoring control and expenditure

There should be a clear pattern for the control of spending. *The LMS Initiative* suggests the following means of control:

1 All expenditure must be authorised by staff with appropriately delegated authority. Staff with responsibility for placing orders should not be able to initiate payment. This will require a separation of duties between teaching staff and administrative support staff.
2 Payment of invoices (with the exception of petty cash) should be through the school's bank account.

(CIPFA 1988)

The use of the computer as part of the record-keeping pattern allows regular monitoring of expenditure. Cave and Wilkinson suggest that the following information should be made available to budget holders on a monthly basis:

- expenditure for the month
- budget for the month
- variance over/under
- total cumulative expenditure to date
- budget to date
- variance over/under

Be responsible for the building and environment

This is normally a responsibility for a senior member of staff. It involves:

Ensuring that the building and the environment are functional for the purposes of the school This means overseeing the work of the care-taking and cleaning staff, which may be a matter of working with the caretaker to deal with the firm supplying cleaning services. It also means ensuring that furniture is in the right place at the right time and seeing that the cleaning and the organisation of the use of the building and grounds are done in such a way that they support the work of the school.

This is more likely to be successful if the caretaker and cleaning staff are kept well informed about the work of the school and if the caretaker is involved in decision making where it affects his work. Teaching staff and students also need to be encouraged to see things from the point of view of the caretaker and his staff and to support their work by being careful.

Seeing that the building and grounds are well maintained The state of the school premises is an important selling point with parents. A school that looks in a bad state of repair is unattractive and not conducive to good work. Staff also look at facilities when accepting appointments and are likely to be drawn to schools where the facilities both for teaching and for the staff are good. It is also false economy to allow the building to fall into disrepair because the costs will eventually have to be met, as many LEAs have discovered. It is therefore worth spending money on the building even in difficult circumstances.

The LEA school's responsibilities for premises will depend to some extent on the delegation formula but all schools are likely to be responsible for furnishing, minor repairs and alterations, although they may have to accept a contract negotiated by the LEA for maintenance of the grounds and for cleaning. Building maintenance may or may not be delegated. They are also responsible for energy costs, water, rents and the council tax. They need to see that the necessary insurance is allowed for and that it covers everything the governors wish it to cover. This may be undertaken by the LEA but the cover which this allows should be checked. The LEA may also charge for the service. The governors are also responsible for health and safety, and arrangements must be made to check on this regularly.

Planning for work on the premises needs to be long-term with plans made for several years ahead, which is difficult when the amount of money coming in is not assured and may be cut. It should nevertheless be given a high priority when money is available. It is a good idea to have a small amount of money reserved for minor repairs but it will be necessary to get competitive estimates for more major work.

Creating an attractive environment   If students are to care about their environment it needs to be interesting and attractive and both students and teachers need to be involved. An environment committee of staff and students may provide ideas about what is wanted to make the school a pleasant place. There should be changing exhibitions of students' work on show in different parts of the building. Students and teachers may also have ideas about making the outside environment interesting and pleasant, perhaps by designing areas for different activities.

Ensuring that there are adequate systems for selecting, storing, maintaining and using materials and equipment   The budget must allow each year for the purchase of some major items of equipment. In some cases it will be possible, and perhaps preferable, to rent equipment. In this case, the agreement should be carefully considered since some schools have found themselves in difficulties when they no longer needed a piece of equipment. The basic questions to ask about equipment being purchased are about product and price. It is also important to consider whether there would be a hiatus in the use of the equipment if a particular member of staff left. Rolph suggests that the following questions may also be useful:

- Will the equipment use other materials?
- Does it have to be serviced at regular intervals?
- Are there any legal implications?
- Will staff have to be trained?
- Can the equipment be stored?
- Are there any security implications?
- Are there enough power sockets?
- Are any other supplies required, for example, water, mains drainage?
- In the case of large and bulky equipment, can we get it into the proposed room and will the floor loadings stand it?'

(Rolph 1990)

A further point to consider is whether there are any safety implications and how these will be met. It may be helpful to get expert advice before purchasing and if possible to visit another school where the equipment is in use.

Rolph also suggests some points to consider in relation to security practice:

- the identification of visitors coming on site
- how the equipment is stored when not in use
- security measures when the equipment is in use
- how equipment issues and loans are managed
- whether the premises are protected by alarms when unoccupied
- who holds the keys to equipment and material storage areas
- whether duplicate keys can be obtained readily
- joint use of premises outside school hours
- whether the equipment has been marked to show ownership
- arrangements at holiday time
- responsibility and liability for equipment taken off site

Space is sometimes taken up in schools because things are badly stored. Different kinds of material and equipment require different kinds of storage. The right storage takes up the minimum of space and makes the materials or equipment easily and immediately available. It also takes into account the need for security both against theft and against injury. A good technology workshop often provides excellent examples of this with tools, equipment and materials stored conveniently. These principles for storage apply equally to other departments.

A second important point about storage is that a combination of storage and records must enable any teacher to see what is available. Teachers of each subject need open access to lists of what is available.

The school not only needs to build in maintenance of certain items of equipment on a regular basis but also needs systems for reporting and dealing with minor breakages and deficiencies.

Each collection of materials and equipment needs a system for withdrawing items for use. This needs to be done in such a way that everyone knows where things have gone and for how long.

Ensure conformity with health and safety legislation

Governors have a legal duty to be concerned with health and safety in school. Doe reminds us that

> where the local authority continues to be the employer (in county and controlled schools) it remains responsible under the Health and Safety at Work Act (1974) for safeguarding employees and persons, such as students, who may be affected but who are not employees.
>
> (Doe 1992)

Governors in aided, independent and grant-maintained schools also bear these responsibilities and all governors have a responsibility for seeing that the school is managed safely. Teachers and other employees must also keep to advice on health and safety in managing their work. The school needs a health and safety policy and a health and safety representative on the staff.

Governors need to check on the following:

1 Are there any hazards in the school building arising from maintenance?
2 What are the arrangements in case of fire?
3 What arrangements are there for the storage and disposal of dangerous substances?
4 Is workshop and laboratory practice being carried out safely?
5 Are there dangers arising from vehicle movement which could be avoided?
6 Are there any hazards arising from cleaning arrangements?
7 Are there any hazards in the playground areas or the grounds generally?

8 What arrangements are being made for safety on school transport or on buses transporting students to and from school?
9 If there are contractors on the premises, what arrangements are being made for the safety of teachers and students?
10 Are accidents being properly reported?
11 Is there adequate provision for first aid?
12 Is there staff involvement in health and safety through staff representatives?
13 Are students being given safety training where this is appropriate?

In addition, heads of department need to be responsible for safe working within their departments and all staff need to be aware of the school health and safety policy.

Chapter 10

Pastoral care and discipline

The care and control of students is a major part of the school's work. It is partly undertaken as a by-product of the learning and teaching programme with all teachers concerned about the individual students they teach, but the size of secondary schools requires an organisation which ensures that responsibility for this area of the school's work is clearly assigned.

The management tasks are as follows:

1 Establish a philosophy of care and discipline.
2 Create and maintain a system for pastoral care.
3 Create and maintain a system for discipline.
4 Ensure the social and personal development of all students.
5 Create and maintain record keeping systems.

Establish a philosophy of care and discipline

Most parents, in seeking a school for their children, are anxious to ensure that it has a suitable balance between the pursuit of academic goals and the care of individual students. In practice these should be complementary, with all members of staff demonstrating concern about individuals in all aspects of their work, but there is also a need to ensure that the necessary elements in the pastoral care programme are visible and properly undertaken. A school needs a policy for pastoral care which spells out:

- the general attitudes expected from staff, students and their parents
- who is responsible for keeping an overview of the development and progress of the individual student and how this will be done

– how personal and social development is to be supported
– the records to be kept and how they are to be used

This policy needs to be widely disseminated and must be accepted by staff, students and their parents. This is more likely if all groups have been involved in some way in drawing up and agreeing the policy.

Create and maintain a system for pastoral care

There is a variety of possible systems for pastoral care and it depends on the particular composition of the school which is the most suitable. Most schools divide students into form or tutorial groups, each cared for by a form tutor. The form group has the following functions:

1 It provides a psychological and physical base for individual students and creates a sense of belonging, particularly when students come new to the school from primary schools where they have been accustomed to being in one class.
2 It provides a channel of communication.
3 It provides a means of maintaining an overview of each student's development and progress.
4 It enables each student to be known well by someone.
5 It offers a channel for fostering individual personal and social development.

The group can be formed in various ways. Some schools mix students so that each tutorial group consists of students from all year groups or from two or three year groups. Mixed age grouping has the advantage that new students settle into a group which is a going concern and in which standards have been established and where there are models of work and behaviour for the younger students. Older students can help to support the teacher and all of them have experience of leading younger students and helping them. Teachers too have experience of the needs of different year groups. A mixed age group may also be easier to manage and control.

There are also disadvantages. If the standards and models are unsatisfactory it will have a negative effect and perpetuate low standards. Older and younger students may have little in common and the older students may make life difficult for the younger ones. The teacher may find the breadth of the task somewhat daunting and do it less well than the teacher who specialises in dealing with the intake year or Year 11. The mixed age group is a less useful communication channel because messages will often be for part of it only. Younger students get less chance of leadership than they do in a single age group form.

Mixed age pastoral groups are often associated with a house structure which involves students from each age group in each house. These may be linked with form groups in which there are students from each house or there may be an organisation where in each year there are forms belonging to each of the houses. The house group then becomes the vehicle for pastoral care and for various kinds of competition. This organisation has many of the advantages and disadvantages of the mixed age pastoral group.

A single year group organisation brings together academic and pastoral organisation. It is a good unit for communication since much of the academic information will apply to everyone. It also has some advantages since teachers can specialize in the needs of a particular year group and become expert at this, although thought should be given to their professional development and opportunities provided for experience of different age groups.

On the other hand the models available to students are more limited. Standards and behaviour have to be established afresh each year. Not all students will get experience of leadership and teachers may not get the experience of dealing with different year groups.

Whichever pattern is eventually chosen, the school needs a staffing structure to match it. Not all teachers are good form tutors and unless the school is very lucky in its staff, it is inevitable that some groups will have form tutors who are less able to perform this task than others. Teachers normally have little preparation in their training for this role and it is the responsibility of management to see that form tutors have sufficient training to be able to undertake it. It can be helpful if inexperienced teachers are able to understudy an experienced form teacher and it also allows tasks to be shared.

One further point which needs to be decided in a single year group organisation is whether form teachers move up the school with their groups. There are many advantages in this. Teachers get to know their groups really well and the students know them. They can take care of continuity between year groups. Each teacher learns the tasks for each year group, but this has the same disadvantage as the mixed tutor group organisation in not providing specialist knowledge of such tasks as linking with primary schools or guiding students in choosing options or careers. Another disadvantage of this pattern is for those students who have the weakest form teachers. Some schools have established a half-way stage with the form tutor staying with the group for two or three years.

The responsibilities of the form tutor will vary to some extent from school to school, but one common intention of the form tutor organisation is that each student should be well known to someone. The following responsibilities are also common:

- administrative tasks relating to the group;
- induction of the students into the school or the year group;
- oversight of the academic progress of each student. The form tutor should be the person who looks at the achievement of each student across the curriculum;
- support for the personal and social development of each student and advice on any aspect of school life and work.

Form tutors may also have responsibilities in terms of overall discipline. The pastoral system needs leadership as well as good form tutors. There may be a structure in which there are heads of year and heads of upper and lower school, or in a house system, heads of house or some other coordinating system. There is something to be said for the appointment of heads of upper and lower school if the school is not too large because of the possibilities for continuity this offers. The role of the pastoral leader should involve:

1 Leading the group of form tutors. This includes any necessary training and development of their skills, advising them on the students in their groups, suggesting and fostering ideas about ways of helping students to develop.
2 Serving as a link in the communication chain, ensuring that form tutors are kept informed and keep their students informed of all relevant information and that there is upward communication to senior management from form tutors' discussions with their students and form tutors' views on relevant issues.
3 Maintaining any programme of learning and development which is undertaken within tutor groups.
4 Ensuring that adequate records are kept, maintained and used.
5 Helping to deal with serious problems.
6 Linking with parents and outside agencies such as psychologists, police, probation service, health service.

It should be noted that the work of the pastoral leader should be judged at least in part on how well the form tutors do their job.

Create and maintain a system for discipline

Young people are growing up in a difficult and confusing world where values and standards vary very considerably and where it is no easy task in many situations to decide right from wrong. While they need and usually welcome a firm but flexible framework for behaviour, they also need to be made as independent and self-disciplined as possible and this will not happen in a school which runs in an authoritarian way. A person needs some freedom if he or she is to learn the process of making personal choices and decisions.

The discipline of any school is heavily dependent upon the establishment of group norms and expectations. It is essential that each new group of students and their parents are led to accept as far as possible the school ethos and preferred modes of behaviour. This means that the preferred behaviour must be continually fostered, explained and be seen by students and parents to be appreciated and rewarded.

There is also a need for discussion among staff about the issues related to social behaviour and a consistency of treatment of students as far as possible. A school needs a clearly recognised policy and system for discipline. This should cover the philosophy of engendering self-discipline and what teachers are expected to do to foster it. It should also give a positive view of what is expected by way of behaviour and the responsibility of teachers for seeing that it is achieved. This should include consideration of ways in which good behaviour is to be rewarded as well as the sanctions to be used for non-conforming behaviour. There should then be a philosophy of ways of dealing with students who break the rules and a clear picture of the attitudes expected from staff as well as statements about rewards and sanctions. It is particularly important to remember that students' misdemeanours offer opportunities for learning and wherever possible teachers should have this in mind. Inexperienced teachers in particular need to feel supported in dealing with any discipline problems they meet and should not feel it a sign of weakness to call on more senior members of staff to support them. At the same time they need to be clear what they are expected to demand from students by way of classroom behaviour and may need support in finding ways of achieving this. Any teacher experiencing difficulty with a student should know exactly what to do if the problem becomes too difficult to handle. The individual teacher needs to know the answers to the following questions:

1 *To whom can I turn immediately for help?* The answer to this question may differ from school to school but is most likely to be the head of department or head of year. The first level of help should not normally be too senior, since more senior staff need to be held in reserve for more serious situations.

2 *At what point should I turn for help?* Inexperienced teachers tend to feel it is an admission of weakness to ask for help but a teacher is more likely to learn how to deal with difficult students if he or she turns to someone experienced at an early stage and later has the chance to talk the incident over, looking for ways in which a different approach might have made things easier.

3 *What sanctions can I use?* Sanctions and punishments tend to be seen as something of a lifeline for the inexperienced teacher while the good experienced teacher hardly needs them. A school system of sanctions is needed and teachers need to know exactly where they stand in relation to them.

A further question which needs to be considered is how discipline incidents are to be recorded in such a way that those responsible for individual students hear about them. One way of doing this is to use duplicate pads on which the teacher referring a student to someone else writes a brief note of the incident with a copy to the form tutor.

The smooth working of a school depends to a great extent on the level of control exercised by teachers. The ideal is that students should be self-disciplined and there should be constant concern to find ways of achieving this. Research suggests that the most effective schools are those where there is a clearly recognised school culture and climate which governs much of what is done (Reynolds 1985, Reid *et al.* 1987, Mortimore *et al.* 1988, Beare *et al.* 1989). This was discussed in Chapter 6 (see pp. 75–83).

It must be recognised that in any society there will be those who are not prepared to fit in and in a secondary school these students can pose considerable problems. There are often groups, usually of boys, although in recent years of girls also, who create a counter-culture in which success is to do things which are contrary to the school culture. There is no easy answer to working with these groups but the following have been found to work in some schools with some students:

1 Have a consistent staff policy about ways of dealing with such students. The staff need to agree on the best way of coping with students of this kind and be consistent in what they do.

2 Ensure that as few students as possible join the disruptive group. Very often, although not always, these groups consists of students who see themselves as failing and it is important to ensure that all students feel they have some success at their own level and that their dignity as people is respected. It can be salutary over a period to check the students who do and do not receive praise and those who receive negative comments. This often shows that some students get nearly all negative comments and few positive ones. It is wise to make this kind of check at an early stage in the school so that teachers are aware of the need to see that certain students do not develop counter-cultural attitudes.

3 Involve the student's parents. For many students, a letter to parents is something which gives them cause for concern and the involvement of some parents may mean that home and school can work together to help a young person through a difficult period. In other cases the parents may be on the side of the students and not prepared to support the school. It is helpful if the school has made good contacts with parents from the early stages so that the relationship is already made when parents are called in to discuss the problems their child is posing. Letters to parents can also be used in a more positive way as a reward for good work or behaviour and there is some evidence that this is an effective way of encouraging students (Harrop and McCann 1983).

4 Make a contract, if possible with an employer involved, that the student will be found a job on leaving school if he or she conforms to some agreed rules, or use work experience or part-time work as an incentive immediately before leaving school. This may not be possible in an area of of high un-employment although it may be possible to find other rewards which would have meaning in this context.

5 Study the situations in which such students create disruption in the class and about the school and look at how these can be avoided. A group of teachers listing the situations where there have been problems, often find that certain incidents trigger off disruptive behaviour and some can be avoided by working in different ways. It is also helpful to teachers to work together to think about appropriate reactions. Teachers feel happier about their problems if they can be shared in a situation which does not suggest weakness on their part.

6 Use a form of behaviour modification. In this context teachers make a point of praising those students who are conforming in behavioural terms as well as in their work. The teacher also works with students who are disruptive to set targets for them such as working for a given (short) time without interrupting anyone else. If such targets are set, it is important that success in achieving them is noted immediately and charted somewhere, so that the student can actually see the progress he or she is making. There is very useful material on this for secondary schools in *Positive Teaching: the Behavioural Approach* (Wheldall and Merrett 1984).

7 Use counselling. This is what most schools do but some students need more skilled counselling than others. There are usually some members of staff who are particularly competent at dealing with such students and it may be helpful to give them time to talk through with difficult students the problems they have and are posing. Teachers of students in schools for behaviourally disturbed children find that making a good relationship with a caring adult is often a help.

Lawrence *et al.* make a number of suggestions, some of which may be helpful:

- Try to nip the incident in the bud.
- Be alert as to how you are feeling. Try not to overreact because you are in a mood – or perhaps not feeling well.
- Don't be precipitated into a confrontation. Deal with an incident on your own grounds when you know exactly how you are going to handle it.
- Avoid over-rigid school sanction structures. There should be plenty of scope for the exercise of discretion.
- It is sometimes possible to diffuse situations by using humour.
- Where a student is a persistent nuisance in lessons, discuss this outside the classroom and discover if possible what lies behind the behaviour.
- Try to avoid becoming personally involved to the point where you thoroughly dislike the student.
- Avoid stigmatising a student for previous delinquency or bad behaviour – it may be better not to know about this.
- It may be helpful if timetablers do not give one teacher too many periods with the same difficult group in the same day, unless the intention is to have a more integrated programme for them.

(Lawrence *et al.* 1984)

If, in the end, none of the ways in which the school tries to help and support a young person who is posing problems to the school works, or if he or she behaves in a way which is totally unacceptable, it may be necessary to suspend that student. Suspension or exclusion may be for an indefinite period, for a fixed term or permanently. Taylor draws on the Education Act No. 2 1986 and DES circular 7/87 para 5.12 and Schedule 3 to provide a statement which sets out the law in such cases:

- Any exclusion of more than three days (or five days in any one term) must be reported to the governors and to the the local authority.
- Parents can make representations to the governors against the exclusion.
- Governors or the LEA can direct that students excluded for more than three days (or five in any one term) or permanently, be reinstated.
- If no date is set for the ending of an indefinite exclusion the LEA must set one.
- If the headteacher decides to make an exclusion permanent, the parents can make a formal appeal to the governors.
- The governors (or a committee of governors set up for that purpose) must hold a formal hearing about a permanent exclusion whether or not the parents appeal.
- If the governors support the headteacher the LEA must, in county schools, decide whether or not to support their decision.
- If the exclusion is confirmed, the parents can appeal to an independent tribunal set up in the same way as the admissions appeals committees.
- If the LEA overrules the governors and reinstates a student, the governors can appeal to the independent committee against reinstatement.
- In voluntary aided schools, the LEA cannot overrule the governors decision to exclude permanently, but parents can still appeal to an independent committee.

(Taylor 1992)

Ensure the social and personal development of all students

Personal and social development has always been a concern of good schools and most schools had a programme of personal and social development in place before the advent of the National Curriculum and its suggestion that personal and social education should be one of the cross-curricular themes. The National Curriculum paper suggests that

> The themes are concerned with the physical, sexual, moral, social and vocational self but subjects of the National Curriculum, religious education, additional subjects and extra-curricular activities . . . also play their part. How the curriculum is managed, its organisation and the teaching methods deployed, the unique combination of factors which create the ethos of a school – its aims, attitudes, values and procedures – all make an important contribution to personal and social education in schools.
>
> The education system is charged with preparing young people to take their place in a wide range of roles in adult life. It also has a duty to educate the individuals to be able to think and act for themselves, with an acceptable set of personal qualities and values which also meet the wider social demands of adult life. In short, the personal and social development of students is a major aim of education; personal and social education being the means by which this aim is achieved.
>
> (National Curriculum Council 1990)

Today's world poses many problems for young people. Drugs, sexual behaviour and a consumer society create pressures which were not present in the past and students need personal strength to avoid pitfalls. Personal and social education involves helping young people to think where they stand on many issues. This learning should be taking place in most areas of the curriculum but it is important that there is a clear understanding of responsibility for teaching particular areas of work. Some may be the form tutor's responsibility; some a part of religious education; some may involve drama; some may arise out of literature studied in the English course and so on. There may also be a specific social and personal education course.

Dean *et al.* describe the work of three schools in attempting to find a way of helping students to set and achieve their own goals. The work started in one school with a multi-choice questionnaire which helped students to identify goals which they wished to achieve and went on to find ways in which they could be helped to plan towards their achievement and evaluate success (Dean *et al.* 1984).

The work which takes place is likely to cover some of the following topics, depending upon the age group of the students:

- settling into the new school; finding your way about; learning what to do; making friends;
- study skills; planning your time and work; homework; revision and examinations;
- social skills; getting on with other people, both adults and peers; how to behave in particular situations; male/female relationships;
- communication skills;
- group norms and the way we are influenced;
- health education; misuse of drugs, smoking, alcohol, fitness, nutrition, personal hygiene;
- education for parenthood;
- sex education including the roles of the sexes in society;
- racism and the need to avoid stereotyping;
- authority and responsibility; the law; crime prevention;
- economic and industrial understanding;
- money management;
- personal interests;
- career guidance.

The pastoral staff of the school, because of their concern with individual students, may often be the people who link with parents and outside agencies such as psychologists, social workers, probation officers and police.

Create and maintain record keeping systems

A child's education should be a continuous and coherent process. Teachers who have overall responsibility for particular students should be able to see what they are studying now as part of a long-term process and have clear records of what has been done at previous stages. The National Curriculum makes this easier than it was in the past.

Teachers should have a general idea of what each student knows and can do within a broad framework and should also be able to differentiate between abilities in different aspects of work in a subject. There is generally too little attention given to the diagnosis of gaps and difficulties in learning in the early years in secondary schools except for those students whose difficulties are serious. The results of the SATs will in future provide this kind of information.

The advent of records of achievement has changed the way in which many secondary schools record students' progress and has provided an opportunity for students to contribute to their own records. The DES report on the progress of records of achievement suggests that 'they should contribute to students' personal development and progress by improving their motivation, providing encouragement and increasing their awareness of strengths, weaknesses and opportunities' (DES 1984).

The process of setting goals by student and teacher as part of the profiling activity is particularly valuable. It helps students to feel in charge of their own progress and makes clear the direction in which they are going.

The overall student records need to give some background information about each student, giving factual information about home and family and previous education. This information might be best collected by asking parents to complete details when the child is admitted to the school. This information can then be set alongside the records coming from the primary school. There should then be a system for entering into the record notes of significant events, possibly in a form which can be removed later. Reports to parents are also part of this process. These are discussed further in Chapter 15 (see pp.210–11).

Chapter 11

Managing people

Management in schools is primarily about managing people. All teachers have to manage children but the management of a school is concerned also with managing adults so that the work gets done. This can be divided into four broad areas:

1 Lead and motivate staff.
2 Delegate effectively.
3 Deal effectively with staff problems.
4 Have knowledge of relevant legislation.

Lead and motivate staff

Margerison, writing about advisory work in industry, lists a number of different kinds of influence:

1 *Force influence*: people in senior positions can influence because of their power to make things difficult if other people do not do as they wish. This influence is there whether or not the person influencing wishes to work this way and it is important to take it into account because people may not show their true reactions to those in power. The problem in exercising force influence is that those being influenced in this way may not be convinced of what they are being asked to do and may therefore do it very superficially.
2 *Knowledge influence*: influence also arises from the skill, knowledge and expertise of the person influencing.
3 *Reward influence*: headteachers are in a position to reward people for moving in certain directions. The reward could be in support for promotion or in provision of materials and equipment for further development of good work or it could simply

be in terms of praise and recognition for work well done. If the school pay policy includes performance-related pay it could include additional pay.

4 *Positional influence*: senior and middle management staff in a school have influence because of the positions they hold. This is akin to force influence and has the same advantages and disadvantages.

5 *Personal friendship influence*: people are influenced by those whom they like and respect. From this point of view it is important to win over the opinion leaders in school when change is contemplated because of the influence they can bring to bear.

(Margerison 1978)

Other types of influence include:

(a) *Persuasion*: this relies on reasoning and is usually the preferred method of influencing others.

(b) *Exchange*: this is really a form of bargaining in which A offers B something in exchange for acting in a certain way. It happens, for example, when the headteacher offers extra resources in order to get a department to update its work.

(c) *Ecology*: it is possible to influence people through their environment. Thus a teacher might be influenced by being next door to another teacher working in a certain way. Teachers may also be influenced to work differently if their working conditions are updated, making it easier to do certain things.

(d) *Magnetism*: this is an aspect of charisma. People are influenced by those who have some kind of drawing power for others.

The human need for satisfaction in relating to other people and for achievement is very important. Many people rate these above salary in their list of requirements in their jobs, although salary will take priority if it is not seen to be a fair reward for work done. Over three decades ago Herzberg wrote of a study in which two hundred engineers and accountants were interviewed about events at work which had either resulted in a marked improvement in job satisfaction or had led to a marked reduction. The major findings of this study showed that strong determiners of job satisfaction were achievement, recognition, work itself, responsibility and advancement, the last three being of greater importance for a lasting change of attitudes. The major dissatisfiers were company policy and administration, supervision, salary, interpersonal relations and working conditions. The dissatisfiers he named the 'hygiene factors' (Herzberg 1959). The findings of this study still have relevance for managers in all kinds of organisations.

Teachers and other members of staff may vary in what motivates them and anyone planning staff development must take this into account. Motivation will probably operate differently at different periods of a person's career and men and women tend to differ in some aspects of what motivates them. Knowledge of the motivating forces is valuable in helping individuals and in thinking out how to provide a programme which will be effective for as many people as possible.

Teachers may be motivated by:

– students developing and learning
– enthusiasm for subject matter
– recognition, praise, interest and encouragement
– a chance to contribute and to shine
– a chance to take responsibility
– a challenge to professional skill
– the inspiration of others
– career prospects

Other staff may be motivated in somewhat similar ways. The stimulus of the content of their work and the students can be an active ingredient in the motivation of ancillary staff as well as teachers.

Leadership behaviour

The various ways outlined above in which people can be motivated come down in the end to the way the leader of a group behaves towards others who are part of it. Leadership behaviour is in the first instance part of personality and most good leaders act instinctively without thinking about how they are operating. But just as teaching behaviour is partly a matter of personality and partly learned, so is leadership behaviour. A leader has various tasks to undertake. The way they are carried out affects the extent to which others are prepared to follow and be influenced.

Many of the characteristics of the effective headteacher listed in Chapter 1 (pp. 3–4) are relevant to the management of people and the following additional points should be noted. The effective leader:

Makes others feel secure Some people in leadership roles create an atmosphere of security from an early stage because of their personalities. However, every leader must eventually earn the trust of colleagues through performance. Security is created through predictable behaviour. People like to know where they stand and how someone is likely to react. They need to know the issues in which their leader wishes to be involved and those which can be left to other people. This does not mean that a leader should always behave in expected ways but that he or she must first satisfy some of the expectations of those being led. Security also comes from the other items on this list.

Is consistent in behaviour Consistency in behaviour is important in creating security and predictability. There must be seen to be rational principles behind a leader's decisions. Every decision made in the early days is creating a precedent for the future. No decision can be taken in isolation.

Is seen to be fair in dealing with people This is another aspect of consistency. A leader must be seen to treat people impartially and normally make the same decision in a similar situation for one person as for another.

Shows support, interest, recognition, praise and encouragement to individuals A leader in any organisation has to do more by way of praising and encouraging than seems obvious and it must be done consistently and impartially. Over a period, the leader needs to demonstrate interest in all staff and offer them encouragement. In many schools where there is dissatisfaction staff will say that no one takes an interest in them.

Is honest One of the most important factors in managing people is the creation of trust. This is not easy because to get trust a person has to give trust and there is risk in this. Trust is most likely when people know that a person will be honest with them in a supportive way. This means saying what is meant but following it up with an offer of support and some genuine steps that the person can take. It is also important not to promise anything which cannot be carried out. It is better for a leader to err on the cautious side and then surprise people by being better than his or her word than to promise and have to go back on this. Trust is also important in obtaining openness. A headteacher who wants staff to explore ideas has to create a situation in which people feel that they can say what they think without being afraid that it will be held against them or that readiness to explore an idea will be taken to mean agreement with it and a readiness to see it implemented.

Is flexible and adaptable   Flexibility in a leader and readiness to have a change of mind if convinced that he or she is wrong are a sign of strength not weakness. What is needed is an ability to stand back from a decision and assess it according to principles.

Delegate effectively

Many people taking on a leadership role for the first time have difficulty in accepting that their task is no longer to do the work themselves but to get it done by others. Headteachers and others in senior posts are often tempted to take on tasks because they know that they can do them well, when the tasks are really the province of somebody else. This means that they are using time which should be spent in other ways and taking up opportunities which others may need to acquire and practise skills.

It is very important to be able to delegate. Delegation provides ways of sharing work equitably. It provides training for staff to develop in their existing posts and an opportunity to prepare for more demanding management roles. In a school where there is much delegation, there are often good candidates for promotion when vacancies occur. It should be part of the professional development programme. A leader who delegates is able to spend more time on evaluation and planning, two aspects of management which can be neglected when pressures build up. He or she can also spend time on those areas of work where attention is most needed. Leaders who delegate and have trained colleagues to take responsibility know that work will continue to be done well in their absence. Headteachers who are frequently pursued by telephone calls when they attend meetings out of school should question whether they are delegating satisfactorily.

When tasks and responsibilities are delegated, sufficient authority must also be delegated. A leader delegating authority must make it clear to everyone concerned that a specified person has been asked to undertake a task or tasks or to shoulder certain responsibilities and that he or she will be supported publicly.

It can be helpful to any leader, even one who delegates well, to analyse the way he or she is spending time and to consider whether enough is being delegated. Details of ways of analysing the use of time are given in Chapter 17 (pp. 234–6). It may also be helpful to work through the following programme:

1 Make a diary analysis for the previous month (or as far back as can be remembered sufficiently well) listing all the tasks under-taken personally. Add any other regular personal tasks and then mark each item with one of the following graded categories:

A   a task which must be done by the holder of the leader's post. This should be done stringently and only tasks which cannot be avoided should be graded A;

B   a task which is done by the leader because he or she has particular skill and knowledge which at present no one else can offer;

C   a task which requires the leader's skill and knowledge but which could be done by somebody else, with help if necessary;

D   a task which ought to be done by somebody else.

2 Review all the tasks listed under D and plan to delegate any likely to recur. Then review the tasks under B and C and con-sider which should be delegated.

3 Discuss the possibility of delegating B tasks with likely members of the team and make plans for delegating them when staff have acquired the requisite skills.

4 Consider whether any of the C tasks can be delegated.

One sometimes hears people say that they cannot delegate a task because they do not feel that it will be done properly. People who say this are often unaware that they are admitting their own failure as managers. It is the manager's job to train others to do a job adequately, not to do it for them. This involves working towards full delegation, helping and supporting the person concerned until he or she can work independently.

Stages involved in delegation

1 *Define the task* A leader delegating for the first time would be wise to set down exactly what is wanted in terms of the outcomes and the limits of the tasks.

2 *Talk it through* Discover with the person concerned how he or she intends to work. It is good practice to ask him or her to go away and think out how to do the job and then to come back and discuss it. This enables the person delegating to check that everything has been thought of and to feed in suggestions.

There is also a need to determine the proposed programme of action. Many tasks require a timetable. Ask for dates by which different stages of the task will be accomplished and note these for future reference.

3 *Monitor progress unobtrusively and supportively*

4 *Review what is happening at regular intervals* Delegation involves reporting back at regular intervals and this is an opportunity to discuss what has happened. A wise leader will ask for regular reports until satisfied that the job is being well done. Then occasional reports and checks may be sufficient. The person delegating must develop a reminder system about this since it is important that people know that there will be a check.

It is useful to ask the person concerned for views about his or her performance as the basis for a discussion about development and to make sure at the beginning that a pattern of reporting back is established. If things go badly, it is probably best not to take over the job or give it to someone else unless this is unavoidable, since this may damage the confidence of the person concerned and lose the learning which may take place if he or she tries again.

Evaluating the process should involve sampling what is happening. It is also important when mistakes are made to analyse what went wrong, remembering that errors and failures are a legitimate part of learning. This analysis should be as objective as possible, looking for pointers to the solution of the problem. Vague criticisms are no use for learning and the leader's task is to see that the other person learns and improves in skill. If he or she can be led to see criticism as objective and supportive, concerned with actions rather than personality and leading to development and growth, this is a valuable tool for staff development.

Things may go wrong for many reasons. If the tasks and the responsibilities being delegated have not been defined adequately, they may be misinterpreted, both by the person with the responsibility and by others.

The planning of the task may have been inadequate. It may help to go through it step by step looking for mistakes and omissions. It may then be possible to draw out of it a strategy which could be applied in future situations and to seek an opportunity to let the person concerned undertake a similar task, this time doing the planning with him or her.

It is not unusual for someone enjoying authority for the first time to use it unwisely. In such a case it is important to get the person to see things from other people's point of view and to anticipate the outcomes of certain actions. This may require quite specific discussion about actions which may have upset others, perhaps painting a picture of how they see the situation.

A quite different problem is when nothing gets done. There are all kinds of reasons for this and an assessment of the reasons will influence the way the problem can be tackled. A clear brief and a firm date by which action is required will persuade most people to start work. The person may have been asked to do more than he or she is able, however. If there seems to be difficulty in taking steps towards the necessary action, try making them smaller still.

Discussion of what has happened should lead to discussion of points for improvement and points which might be relevant elsewhere, for sometimes someone coming new to a task discovers ideas or ways of working which might be of interest to others. In such a case the information needs to be appropriately disseminated.

Finally, a leader needs to come back to a personal analysis and look at whether his or her skills in coaching are adequate. Delegation is not easy and the final responsibility is that of the leader. Every time a leader delegates there is a risk, but if there is periodic review he or she will get better at delegating. It is a learning situation for the leader as well as for the person to whom a task is delegated.

Deal effectively with staff problems

Managing people involves dealing with many different kinds of problems. Some of these are personal and need human sympathy and care. Some are professional and involve the competence of teachers. Some are to do with conditions of service of teachers and with various forms of industrial action. Yet others are legal problems arising out of conditions of employment. More recently there have been difficult decisions to make about redundancies. The headteacher of a school is likely to encounter problems of all kinds.

Personal problems

Teachers and other staff may have problems of their own which they bring to school and which colleagues may try to help them solve. A headteacher cannot stand aside from such problems for they may affect the professional work of staff unable to concentrate because they are preoccupied with other matters. In some cases the problem will gradually resolve itself. The marriage will break up and the partners start to make new lives; the illness will move into a period of recovery; the mourning will end. In other cases there will be no solution but a need to cope from day to day, as in the case of parents with a handicapped child. Sometimes the problem is part of the individual's personality and all that anyone can do is listen and support as far as possible. A good deal that is said in the next chapter is relevant here.

It is important in dealing with problems of this kind for headteachers and senior members of staff to keep their own balance. They need to be sympathetic and caring but their first duty is to the rest of the school and hard decisions may have to be taken.

Professional problems

Every headteacher encounters professional problems among the staff. There will be those who fail to pull their weight in more senior posts and those who fail in some degree at all levels.

The first task is to identify the nature of the problem. If anything is to be done about it, it needs to be analysed in some detail. This means going beyond the statement that Jim Smith finds it difficult to handle Year 9 groups of less able students or that Margaret Jones upsets other people when she tries to fulfil her role as head of department in an excessively bureaucratic manner. They need to be observed at work and as much evidence as possible collected which will enable someone to help them.

Part of any problem is the way that people see it. If it is to be resolved it is necessary to know how the problem is viewed generally by those concerned with it. The views people hold may not be accurate but that in itself may be part of the problem. A headteacher may not be made aware directly of these views unless people feel very strongly, but the senior team working together is likely to be well informed about the nature of the problems.

The next step is to get the person concerned to see the problem in a way that allows progress. This may mean working to get him or her to acknowledge that there is a problem or trying to make the problem loom less large in order to generate enough confidence to overcome it. People who have problems in relationships often have difficulty in accepting that the problems are of their own making and it can be useful in these cases to concentrate on suggesting that they try a different approach without necessarily insisting that they acknowledge the problem. Such people often press for details of the evidence which it may not be possible to give. Others refuse to agree that what has happened is in any way their fault when evidence is given.

It is not unusual to find that a school is desperately concerned about the problems a teacher is posing but that no one has actually talked to the teacher directly about them. This is less likely to happen now that we have regular appraisal, but even here problems can be side-stepped. This is mistaken kindness. If someone is failing, it is the task of management to see that everything is done to improve that person's performance. At some stage this means discussing the problems frankly and setting them out in terms which lead to positive outcomes which are unequivocal.

A useful first step is to identify the kind of improvement required in terms that the person concerned can understand and to agree goals which can be seen to be achieved. Thus in dealing with a teacher who is having problems in class because of poor organisation one might ask for written preparation listing what is needed for each lesson with plans for changes of activity. This could then be discussed at a regular weekly meeting with the head of department. In dealing with a teacher in a middle management post who is failing because of personal relations, one possible solution might be to arrange for him or her to attend a course on assertiveness in order to learn how to work more positively with other people.

If these approaches are not successful it may be necessary to consider what further help is needed or what disciplinary action is required. This may still be action from within the school or a headteacher may call in outside help. It may be necessary to involve governors if it seems that disciplinary procedures may be needed, but initially this will be a matter of informing rather than asking for action, since the governors may be required to act in a disciplinary role later.

Where failure continues and, in spite of support and help, is at a level which could be regarded as serious enough to consider dismissal on grounds of incompetence, a headteacher will have to embark on the formal processes leading up to this. This area is covered very thoroughly by employment legislation and it is important to follow procedures correctly. For local authority schools there will almost certainly be procedures laid down and agreed within the authority and it is wise to involve the education office as soon as the situation seems to be serious enough to warrant it, to find out the local practice.

Before moving on to a formal warning it is normal to give a person at least one informal warning that his or her work is unsatisfactory in some respect and to offer help and support for improvement, including both help in school and opportunities for appropriate training. A formal warning must be in writing, setting out how the person must improve and giving a period during which there must be improvement. If the improvement is not sufficient within the time allowed there may be further warnings leading to a final formal warning. The governors may decide to recommend dismissal in the case of a local authority school or to dismiss the teacher themselves in the case of other schools.

At any disciplinary hearing the teacher concerned has a right to be represented with a friend at the governors' meeting. In the case of dismissal there is also a right to appeal subsequently to the education committee in the case of a local authority school and/or to an industrial tribunal. The teacher has the right to receive copies of any reports the headteacher or others may be making to the governors, fourteen days in advance of the meeting. Governors may also be involved in an appeal and those involved in the appeal may not be the same people as those who were involved in the case in the first instance.

A school should have its disciplinary rules for staff in writing as well as those for pupils. These should state the kind of offence which could be regarded as misconduct and the possible penalties.

Where a teacher or other member of staff is failing, the keeping of notes becomes very important. A failing teacher needs to be seen in the classroom regularly by a senior member of staff and the headteacher and these lessons must be recorded in some detail and a note given to the teacher setting out what he or she must do to improve. Discussion should take place while the event is fresh in the observer's mind. It should be remembered in doing this that written statements could become evidence at an industrial tribunal.

Headteachers should, if possible, arrange for someone outside the school, such as an adviser or inspector, to see the teacher in question. The presence of a senior member of staff in the classroom changes the situation and students are likely to behave better simply because the senior person is there. It is also difficult for a senior member of staff to allow a serious level of bad behaviour to continue unchecked. This problem is less likely when the visitor is unknown. Headteachers in grant-maintained schools may like to invite a colleague from a neighbouring school to act in this capacity.

It is also important to remember that a tribunal will wish to be assured that procedures have been correctly followed and that everything possible has been done to help and support the teacher. They will look for evidence of work observed and discussed, advice and help given, in-service and other opportunities of various kinds provided. It is therefore important not only to make such help available but to record that it has been done.

A rather different set of problems occurs when a teacher does something which is professionally unacceptable to the point which warrants disciplinary procedures. This would include sexual offences, assault, theft or mishandling of money or other criminal offences and similar matters. In such a circumstance a headteacher may wish to suspend the teacher from duty pending enquiry and inform the governors. Again, for local authority schools, it is important to consult the local office as well as the governors so that the action is correct at each stage. Where a headteacher is in doubt about what to do, the teacher can be sent home while investigations are made. It will eventually be the responsibility of the governors to decide what should be done and, in the case of a maintained school, to make recommendations to the authority.

Relationship problems

A number of problems in school are to do with relationships between people and senior staff may find themselves trying to resolve a problem which is basically one of people not getting on together.

There may be conflicts about territory and who does what. There may be conflicts over ideology where one person does not agree with another person's handling of a situation because it does not conform to his or her frame of reference. There may also be conflict between people who just dislike each other to the point where they find it difficult to work together.

Caldwell and Spinks suggest that agreement in conflict situations might be achieved by getting people to collaborate in the goal-setting process, having considered needs and formulated policies (Caldwell and Spinks 1988). This may well be the best way to deal with conflict over ideology and over the distribution of resources. Many of the conflicts about territory may be resolved by defining more carefully the limits of each person's responsibilities. If there is conflict over territory this probably means that the boundaries are not sufficiently clear.

Conflict can be dealt with in a number of ways:

1 A discussion can be arranged, chaired by the manager concerned, to talk out the problem and arrive at agreed solutions. This is an essential first step in trying to resolve problems.
2 Time can be spent agreeing needs and possible ways of meeting them, going on to agree goals.
3 Rules and procedures can be devised and used or job descriptions revised. This can be a useful way of resolving conflict over territory where the task is to sort out which people are responsible for which activities.
4 The people concerned can be separated if this is possible.

Much of what is said about negotiation in Chapter 12 is relevant here (pp. 160–3).

Have knowledge of relevant legislation

There has been a great deal of employment legislation in recent years as well as other legislation affecting schools. Headteachers need to be aware of the provisions of the following acts:

- The Equal Pay Act 1970 (as amended)
- Trade Union and Labour Relations Act 1974
- Health and Safety at Work Act 1974
- Employment Protection Act 1975
- Sex Discrimination Acts 1975 and 1986
- Race Relations Act 1976
- Employment Protection Acts (consolidation) 1978
- Employment Act 1980
- Employment Act 1982
- Trade Union Act 1984
- Wages Act 1986

- Teachers' Pay and Conditions Acts 1987
- Employment Act 1988

The issue of redundancy is very much with us and each school needs to have a clear and agreed practice for deciding who should go when staff are to be declared redundant. The process must be seen to be fair, although it must also be influenced by who can be spared. Even when it is clear that the specific department could manage with one fewer teacher, the question still arises about which member of the department should go. Probably the most usual principle is 'last in first out' but there certainly need to be criteria, known to everyone, by which the decision is made.

Chapter 12

Interpersonal skills

Success in a senior post or in headship depends very largely on relationships with people. People learn skills in making relationships as they grow up and most people develop these skills further as they progress through middle management to top management posts. However, the tasks a headteacher or senior member of staff is called upon to undertake and the kinds of relationships formed are rather different from those practised at earlier career stages because the role is a different one. Other people also have strong expectations of what someone in the role of headteacher should do and, while it may be a good idea to surprise them occasionally by doing something different, it is necessary to fulfil their expectations if one is to have their trust.

Common features of interpersonal situations

There are common features to most interpersonal situations. They include the following:

The effect of the venue

Environment affects what happens. The way a room is arranged affects interaction. For example, in some situations a headteacher may choose to talk with someone sitting on a level with him or her in an easy chair and this creates a particular kind of relationship. On other occasions it may be politic to stay sitting behind a desk in order to make a different impression and create a different relationship.

People are also affected by the degree of privacy, and inferences are drawn from the place where an interview is conducted. The headteacher's room has overtones which affect reactions in different ways. The headteacher is always more at home there than other people. People will also draw conclusions if a serious interview is constantly interrupted by the telephone or a secretary. It suggests that they are not important enough to be given the headteacher's full attention.

Discomfort interferes with listening and attending to what is going on. If it is difficult to see or hear a speaker, if the seats are uncomfortable or the temperature too hot or too cold, an audience may make little effort. This is also true to some extent in a face-to-face interview, though the content may be of such vital importance that the people concerned attend to the business in hand in spite of discomfort.

The way the interchange starts

The beginning of any interpersonal activity sets the scene for what follows. In a talk the speaker's first words may gain or lose everyone's attention. In an interview or negotiation the scene may be set by the way the senior person makes the other feel at ease or threatened.

Where an interview deals with a difficult topic it is probably best to start with more general conversation and then move into an explanation of the purpose of the interview. If the senior partner wishes to make notes, it is often wise to explain this so that the other person does not feel threatened by it. It is also helpful at an early stage to define what the interview is about. All of this applies to appraisal interviews and to any face-to-face discussion.

The way people react to each other

It is very important to be able to read the body language messages people send which tell how they are reacting to what is being said.

The following signs are common and are relevant when speaking or working with a group as well as in dealing with individuals:

Eye contact We signal the beginnings and ends of exchanges and many other ideas with our eyes. Keeping eye contact in talking to someone is very important if the person concerned is to feel that the conversation is sincere.

Interest, involvement, concern Attention and interest are signalled by eye contact, smiles, nods, sounds of agreement. These are also signalled when someone sits forward.

Tension People show tension by adopting an uncomfortable sitting position; by clenching and unclenching their hands; moving their feet about; by facial expression in which the muscles of face and jaw are tight; frowning; by exhibiting signs of dryness of mouth.

Lack of interest, impatience, boredom These are signalled by losing eye contact, looking at the time, playing with something, sitting back and looking far away.

Embarrassment, anxiety feelings or hurt These may occur in the course of a meeting with an individual or group and it is important to recognise them quickly in order to be aware of what is happening. All the tension signals may also convey emotional involvement. Eye contact may be dropped when the situation is emotionally charged.

Views of relative status People convey messages about status to a greater extent than is usually realised. It is usually possible to recognise very quickly who is the senior person in an interview or discussion. He or she will exercise a degree of control over what is happening, summing up the discussion occasionally and moving to a new topic, perhaps 'talking down' the other person on occasion or using status to dismiss or encourage the other's ideas. The more senior person will speak with a greater degree of con- fidence and authority than other people and may hold eye contact until someone else drops it.

Conversely those who see themselves in more junior positions will reverse these actions, backing down easily when someone else talks them down or retains eye contact. They may put ideas for- ward more tentatively than their senior colleague and it may be his or her role to draw out ideas from them so that they are able to make a contribution.

Presenting material to a group

People in management roles find themselves required from time to time to put something over to a group of adults. The task of communicating with a group varies from one occasion to another in a number of important respects, including group size and composition, subject matter, context and the state of the audience. A speaker can choose from a range of possible approaches to achieve the optimum communication within the particular set of circumstances, choosing subject matter and language for the particular audience and using voice and gesture to stimulate them.

Preparing a talk involves considering the subject matter to be covered, the approximate size and composition of the audience, the time available, the context of the particular talk and the environment in which it will be given. A good beginning captures the audience and makes them feel that the speaker is with them and a good ending sends people away with something to think about. A speaker who has prepared the end of a talk can jump to the end if time is running out although a good speaker should be able to time a talk accurately.

For a person who is frequently giving talks or regularly giving similar talks, it can be useful to prepare notes on cards or on OHP transparencies, in very small units. These can then form the nucleus of materials from which to select for a particular talk. If OHPs are made with water based markers, they can be changed in detail to match a particular talk. Once the outline has been prepared, the use of visual aids or handouts can be considered. These must add to or reinforce what is said as well as providing variety.

Experienced speakers take time over starting and they look at the audience, who at this point are making judgements about whether this speaker will be worth listening to. It is helpful to a speaker to scan the audience, making eye contact with individuals and noting the behavioural clues listed above.

A talk should end with something memorable, perhaps a summing up, a quotation or a story which emphasizes some of the main points.

Talking to an individual

There are many situations in a which a headteacher or senior member of staff has to deal with individual people in a one-to-one situation. He or she may see someone in order to gain information, deal with a problem, counsel, receive or give criticism, make a request, appraise a situation or the work of an individual or for many other reasons. These may all be regarded as interviews.

All interviews call for a high degree of skill. Moreover, many of them have to be dealt with as and when they arise, although some may be programmed.

There are a number of different kinds of interview:

Interviewing for information

Interviewing to obtain information is one of the commonest types of interview. It is also a necessary beginning to interviewing for problem solving, appraisal, counselling and selection and is frequently necessary in its own right.

Interviewing for information involves getting as much accurate information as possible in the shortest time compatible with maintaining good relationships. The task of the interviewer is to create a situation in which information is freely given and to check what he or she is told by asking questions and by offering summaries for comment. It is often valuable to go beyond the facts and try to find out how the other person feels about what he or she is saying. This may give some indication of its accuracy, since people are more likely to misinterpret matters they feel strongly about. It may also offer clues to acceptable action.

Problem-solving interviews

A problem-solving interview involves getting information about the problem, including finding out how people view it, exploring and considering solutions, considering how people are likely to feel about them, and possible action.

The interviewer should make sure he or she has got down to the real problem before starting to explore solutions. A person's feelings about a problem may lead to an illogical description. Minor problems may be used as a route to discussion of major problems and getting to the nub of the real problem may take time.

It is easy for an interviewer to assume that what worked for him or her in a similar situation will work for someone else and suggest this solution at an early stage. Different people work differently and it is wise to be wary of offering solutions too quickly and to try instead to lead people to formulate their own solutions when possible. These are often the most successful.

It is important to preserve a measure of professional detachment. Problems may be emotionally charged and it is essential that someone trying to help is seen as sympathetic yet calm and able to see the problem in perspective.

Many problems come down to issues of behaviour and relationships. Some of these can be eased if the person concerned can identify and agree something to work at as suggested in the last chapter.

Most schools have some problems which are very difficult to solve. In a few cases there are no good solutions. In the majority of cases, however, the situations should be viewed positively, especially where they concern human behaviour. One can reflect that teachers in schools for children with severe learning difficulties achieve results by breaking down tasks into very small steps until they reach a point where the pupil is able to succeed. Each minor success is rewarded with praise and comment and minor successes gradually add up to greater achievement. These techniques can be applied to almost any situation.

Receiving a complaint

One common interview situation which all headteachers and senior staff encounter is that of receiving complaints. A complaint may be against the headteacher or teacher personally or a complaint against a colleague or the school or some part of it. Some people making complaints are aggressive. Others are apologetic and negative, sometimes starting by apologising but then getting increasingly aggressive as they become more emotionally involved. It is easy to respond to this situation by being aggressive or defensive in return. Neither approach is satisfactory.

A few people make complaints all the time but for the most part a situation has to become bad before they voice their concern. Consequently a headteacher may face someone who is in an emotional state and who has rehearsed the scene many times before coming to complain. It is often helpful to encourage the person to talk without interruption until the tale is finished. When the end comes, the story can be filled out and checked by asking questions and running through the information as it has been given.

What happens next depends upon whether the complaint is about something which involves other people and whether the evidence is available. If the evidence is only the story according to the complainant, then, after listening sympathetically, a headteacher may offer to investigate and give the other person some idea of what may be involved, arranging to let him or her know in some way the result of investigations.

If the whole story is there, the listener has to decide on a course of action. If he or she personally is in the wrong to any extent, the best course may be to apologise. A person never loses by apologising when wrong and it is more likely to lead to future good relationships than would a defensive reaction.

Whatever the rights and wrongs of the situation, the person complaining wants to go away feeling that something will happen as a result of complaining. The listener has to decide what this can be.

A difficult situation is when the complaint is against one of the teachers and the headteacher whole-heartedly agrees with the complainant. There is no point in refusing to accept that the teacher is wrong. However, most people accept that a headteacher has to be loyal to the staff and is therefore unlikely to join those complaining about teachers. A parent will normally be mollified by a promise to talk to the teacher concerned about the problem without too much comment about how the headteacher views the incident.

It is always wise to end an interview of this kind with a summary of what has been said and a plan for action on the part of the interviewer and possibly on the other person's part, sometimes following this with a note of what has been agreed.

No one likes receiving complaints, but this is part of the head-teacher's role. However, they can be seen as an opportunity to learn how matters seem as seen from a different viewpoint. The situation then becomes more positive.

Criticising someone's work

All managers from time to time need to be critical of someone else's performance. The way a headteacher or senior member of staff does this will determine whether or not the person concerned leaves the discussion feeling that it is important to do everything possible to improve and that the headteacher or head of department will do everything possible to help, or goes away feeling thoroughly bloody-minded and determined to retaliate at the first possible opportunity. Between these extremes will be the person who feels miserable or defensive about what was said in the discussion but uncertain what ought to be done about it. In this situation a person will probably try to forget an unpleasant incident without doing very much about it. It is therefore important to criticise in a way which brings a commitment to improvement.

It helps if the person criticising can choose the time and place for the discussion. It is easier to discuss a problem when the person concerned does not feel that a reprimand is being fitted in before the person criticising dashes off to deal with something else. The matter is vital to the person being criticised and it is reasonable to expect it to be the same for the person criticising.

It is unwise to criticise someone in front of another person except where a witness is needed or a fellow interviewer can help.

The way a manager conducts such an interview affects the seriousness with which the other person regards it. It is possible to create a relaxed or a formal situation. When a problem first comes to light it is usually best dealt with in a relaxed way, perhaps with both parties seated in easy chairs or at least on the same level. At a later stage it may be necessary to make the situation more formal, but usually the informal methods of dealing with people are more productive.

It is important to think out beforehand how best to run such a discussion. It is particularly important for the person interviewing to be sufficiently in control to avoid expressing feelings unintentionally. The expression of anger, for example, is a tool to be used rarely and deliberately and with considerable forethought about the outcome. 'Tearing someone off a strip' may relieve one's feelings, but is more likely to produce an aggressive response than a desire to improve. Conversely it is necessary to avoid being so gentle and kind that the person is left feeling that the matter is not important. The ideal is to be sympathetic but firm and to state the criticism clearly.

It is important to listen carefully to what the person has to say, questioning to ensure that his or her point of view is understood. It is often a good idea to start by asking for an account of whatever is being discussed from the other person's viewpoint so that both sides can be seen. This not only gives the interviewer a chance to sum up the situation but tends to take the steam out of it, because it can be seen that the interviewer is trying to be fair. People often see their own actions more clearly if asked to describe them and sometimes the other person will say all that is necessary by way of personal criticism. The interviewer's part is then to help the other person to reflect on performance and identify possible action which can be taken. Such an interview should end with an agreed commitment to action and a date for reviewing the situation.

Refusing requests

Saying no is not always easy, but a headteacher who has not learned to recognise the occasions when it is the best answer will rapidly run into difficulties. It is also easy to go to the other extreme and say yes too rarely.

The first task is therefore to define the criteria for saying no, thus providing a yardstick by which to measure requests. The following are possible criteria, although they may need to be modified and extended for a particular situation:

- Does what is requested:
  - further the broad aims of the school?
  - further the headteacher's own aims for the school?
  - further the aims of the individual making the request?
- Is what is requested likely to:
  - take an unreasonable amount of time from other activities?
  - use an unreasonable amount of resources of other kinds?
  - create problems for other people?
- Is what is requested contrary to any agreed policy or practice or in conflict with any other activity?

Saying no is not just a matter of deciding what to do against criteria, but of actually saying it. This can be difficult when someone comes along enthusiastic about a scheme which must be refused because of the problems it poses.

It may be possible to help the person to change the request so that it becomes acceptable. If this is not possible, then it is important to share the criteria so that the person concerned can not only see why the answer is no but can also make this judgement for him or herself on a future occasion.

A further problem for a manager about saying no is to discern the occasion when he or she should have a change of mind after getting further information. It is not a sign of weakness for a person to give way if matters begin to be seen in a different light. On the other hand, if this happens too frequently, other people will not accept an initial no and will spend a lot of time and effort trying to get a different answer. Here again, the criteria are important. If a headteacher can say that he or she is having a change of mind because the request now seems to fit the criteria in a way that it did not before, it makes for rationality all round.

Interviews sometimes go wrong because there is some form of misunderstanding. Words, gestures and movements are misinterpreted and every interviewer should try to check the understanding of the other person by summarising and questioning further.

Sometimes matters go wrong after the interview, when the person concerned has had time to think it over. This is particularly likely if the interview was an emotional one. It is wise to make a note of the content of any interview in which decisions are made or where the content has been emotional or possibly threatening. Notes are best made while the information is fresh in mind and if appropriate a copy sent to the other person so that there is no misunderstanding.

In a situation where an interview is likely to prove threatening in a serious way, for example, giving a member of staff an informal or formal warning, it may be wise to involve a witness. This also provides the possibility of another mind on the problem.

Negotiation

Everyone in a management role spends a good deal of time in negotiation. Negotiation, in this context, is not only negotiation with trade unions or professional associations, but with the day-to-day task of bringing people closer in their views so that profitable action can ensue, of interpreting one person to another and persuading people to work together, of finding a way forward acceptable to everyone.

Negotiating involves a person attempting to understand the frame of reference from which the other person is working and looking at where it matches his or her own. This gives a basis for arguments towards any particular end.

There is a sense in which all leadership has to be negotiated. A teacher in charge of a class is its designated leader but maintains this role by negotiating with the students. One sometimes hears a teacher indulge in a kind of trading with the students, 'When you have finished your writing you may choose an activity.' Occasionally the students ask a question such as 'Do we *have* to do this?' A teacher also has to establish the level of work expected from students and the students try to find out what the teacher will accept. Similarly, teachers and other staff negotiate what is acceptable with the headteacher and senior staff.

There is also negotiation with parents and students about such matters as uniform, homework, rules and discipline. Teachers negotiate who teaches particular groups or parts of the curriculum. The headteacher has many negotiating tasks inside and outside the school. Inside the school the headteacher is continually discussing and agreeing patterns of work, negotiating with teachers, office staff, caretaker, cleaning staff, the caterer and dinner helpers and with union representatives of these groups. Headteachers also negotiate with parents, governors, local authority officers, advisers and inspectors, the local community and employers and others.

Every school has to draw together the philosophy of its head-teacher and staff and the views of parents, governors, students and community, including employers. Aims and objectives will not usually be shared unless a deliberate attempt is made to explain the school's viewpoint, listen to the views of others and take them into account. This involves negotiation.

Teachers negotiate with headteachers and others for the resources of time, materials and accommodation. Headteachers may negotiate with their governors over the use of the resources they have and with parents and sponsors for additional resources.

Students negotiate behaviour with the teacher and teachers negotiate behaviour with the headteacher and senior staff. The school negotiates behaviour with parents and the community. If the community dislikes the behaviour of students, parents will not send their children to the school.

All teachers with a management function in school have to negotiate their role. Generally speaking the headteacher's role is understood and the headteacher may therefore have less nego-tiating to do than some other people. A new headteacher will still need to negotiate a particular way of working, however.

Many deputy headteachers find that they need to negotiate their role, partly because the deputy headteacher's role may be ill-defined, even when there is a clear job description, because it depends upon the management style of the headteacher and what the individual in post has to offer. In the course of a deputy headteacher's first year or two in the school, he or she will be modifying personal views in the light of the views of the head-teacher and colleagues and they will be modifying their views in the light of the deputy's performance, so that the deputy's role eventually becomes acceptable to everyone.

This is the most common use of the word and it includes day-to-day resolving of differences between individuals as well as management/worker or trade union negotiation.

Fisher and Ury describe negotiation as getting what you want from others. They suggest that what is required is what they call principled negotiation. This involves looking for mutual gains and then making decisions about areas of conflict by agreeing standards (Fisher and Ury 1987). For example, a governing body is concerned and doubtful about the way in which students with special needs are being supported in the classroom. They feel that such students should be in a separate group. The staff who have experienced the current way of working are convinced that this is right for these students and that they make better progress both academically and socially when they work with more able groups. It may be possible in this situation to get governors and staff to agree that if it can be shown that these students are making progress suitable to their ability then the staff are probably right in their view. This would mean deciding on and agreeing the criteria by which this would be judged. If, on the other hand, the agreed criteria show that there is substantially less progress than staff thought there would be then perhaps the staff should think again. Fisher and Ury argue that taking positions should be avoided and that discussion should be concentrated first on the areas of agreement and then on the criteria by which decisions about the areas of conflict should be decided. They suggest that the more one knows about the views and feelings of the other party, the more chance there is of resolving the conflict in a way which is satisfactory to everyone.

Negotiation involves much of the thinking about aggressive and assertive behaviour. Back and Back contend that there is a midway between being aggressive, on the one hand, and making only a very limited attempt to express and maintain a point of view (non-assertiveness), on the other. This midway is what is described as assertive behaviour (Back and Back 1982). Assertive behaviour is where an individual states his or her views firmly, clearly and politely in such a way that it evokes a positive response. The right kind of assertive behaviour may also deflect attention from what seems to be an attack on a person, to a supportive analysis of the nature of differences and problems.

Negotiation takes place either between people who are equal in status or where one is senior to the other. It may also be between individuals or among a group. These aspects makes differences of approach necessary in different situations.

Negotiation between equals means that people start with equal rights to be heard and to make the final decision. It may therefore be more difficult to achieve a decision, but all those involved need to make an effort to see the others' viewpoints because they need to understand in order to argue their own views. Sometimes the conclusions reached in these circumstances are good ones where all parties have modified their original views to arrive at consensus. On other occasions, the discussion may take a good deal of time and the outcome may be one that nobody likes or even a stalemate which effectively prevents action. This is what tends to happen in strikes.

This kind of situation is most frequently resolved by a third party who may be a neutral arbitrator (such as ACAS in the industrial setting) or by the involvement of someone more senior.

Negotiation between groups or individuals who are not of equal status also has its problems. Negotiation between the headteacher and a member of staff is conducted in the knowledge that the headteacher has the right to have the last word. The effect of this knowledge on the staff member may be that he or she tests out the headteacher's views and when they appear to differ from his or her own, backs down quickly without pressing a point of view or explaining the ideas sufficiently for the headteacher to assess them adequately. This is something that the senior partner needs to recognise and try to avoid.

Alternatively the member of staff faced with the likelihood that the headteacher will disagree may start to act aggressively and try to pressure the headteacher into agreement. Somewhere between these two forms of behaviour comes the assertive approach which achieves a proper consideration of the issues and an outcome which is acceptable to both parties. This is not to suggest that the headteacher or senior member of staff should keep silent about his or her own views. A headteacher in this situation needs to give a good indication of the parameters within which he or she is prepared to work in such a way as to appear open to new ideas and ways of doing things. This is not easy.

Negotiation does not always go smoothly or have a satisfactory ending. Sometimes one person will manoeuvre another into an impasse, where neither can move without losing face. When discussion takes place in a group, it is the task of the chairperson to resolve this kind of conflict and it is sometimes useful to suggest that the problem is set aside for a while and returned to later, when it is not unusual to find that resolution is easier.

Leading a group

Group leadership is an important part of management. There are
many situations when a leader is expected to take the chair, sometimes formally and sometimes informally.

Although the skills required for leading different kinds of
groups vary from one group to another, the majority are common
to most groups.

Preparation for the meeting

A leader should do some preparation for every meeting. This may
simply be a matter of going through the agenda of a regular
meeting and considering how to deal with each item. If the meeting is one for discussion of a particular topic or topics it may
require the following kind of preparation:

– Study the material for discussion and clarify:
  • the objectives of the discussion;
  • what needs to be put in writing before and during the dis-
    cussion. This may include an agenda, discussion outline,
    members' list, background papers;
  • possible starting points or ways of presenting items;
  • what should be achieved by the end of the meeting;
– Prepare:
  • a plan for getting started. If a meeting has an agenda this will
    not be needed, but where a meeting is concerned with explo-
    ratory discussion the starting point is important;
  • a series of points and questions which need to be covered in
    the course of the discussion;
  • a plan for drawing the meeting to a close, particularly if it is
    an exploratory discussion. A group leader needs to have
    some idea of how far the group might get and of possible
    ways of finishing the discussion;
  • a time plan for discussion. If there is a formal agenda it may be
    useful to put a rough time by each item. It is also wise to set a
    finishing time and make people aware of it before the meeting;
– Consider the venue and seating plan. Discussion can founder if
  people are not comfortably seated so that everyone can see
  everyone else. A circle is usually the best arrangement. Avoid a
  straight line of chairs if possible because people in a line do not
  see each other.

- Decide whether to take notes. Some people find it easy to chair a meeting and take notes but it is usually better to ask someone else to act as scribe and it is wise to arrange this before the meeting. If notes are not taken it can become difficult to sum up and draw conclusions and much of the discussion may be lost.

The working session

The way a group starts work is important. When a group is newly formed, people may have all kinds of views, fears and prejudices, especially if the group and its leader are unfamiliar to each other or participants are overawed by the status of the group leader or some group members.

It is helpful to provide an opportunity for each person to speak as soon as possible and reward each contribution with some kind of acknowledgement – a smile or nod or comment. The leader needs to see that the task of the group is clearly stated and understood and to watch for those who are ready to speak. During the discussion the leader's main task is that of controlling the discussion and drawing together the thinking of the group. This means that he or she needs to:

- Set and maintain the rules of discussion. In a formal meeting the rules are laid down and the chairperson has to see that they are followed, establishing the extent to which he or she is prepared to allow divergence from the task in hand, recounting of anecdotes, discussion between sections of the group and so on. In an exploratory group it is possible to be more flexible than with a more formal group with an agenda.
- Maintain a relationship with each member of the group by the way he or she reacts to contributions. The leader's skill in questioning and extending contributions, rewarding them in various ways and his or her interest in what members say, does much to determine the readiness with which people speak and the degree of frankness they offer. The leader should try not to talk too much.
- Scan the group from time to time, looking round to see those who may wish to speak. Someone may be trying to catch the eye of the group leader or is perhaps sitting forward or in the process of drawing breath to speak. The leader should look for anyone who appears to be bored or detached or becoming

interested in something outside the discussion and draw that person back in.

- Maintain the direction of the discussion by extending contributions and relating them to the task in hand, looking for trends and directions in what people say or patterns in the contributions. The leader needs to be analysing and classifying what is being said so that he or she gradually helps the group to create a coherent body of thought.

- Sum up and move the discussion on when it seems the right moment to do so. The leader needs to make the group aware at intervals of the direction of the discussion, perhaps summing up points of agreement and difference at the apparent conclusion of a section of discussion. There is a right moment to do this. A group which is not ready to move will usually refuse to start thinking of anything else until they are ready to change direction. Where there is a formal agenda the chairperson may need to sum up the findings of each item.

- Deal with any problems arising. For example, the leader needs to be on the look out for silent or over talkative members and draw the former into the discussion and find ways of ensuring that the latter gives others a chance to speak. There may be cases of conflict or emotional tension where the leader has the choice of talking this through or alternatively changing the direction of the group. The leader's decision depends upon whether it seems to be worth the trouble of working through the conflict and whether he or she feels able to handle it.

A group sometimes decides that it does not wish to work at the task in hand, and its members will introduce red herrings, act negatively or helplessly and refuse to think constructively. This kind of behaviour has to be worked through but there will eventually be a moment when the group is ready to move if the leader keeps trying to get its members going in a constructive way. Where a leader knows this is likely to happen it may be a good idea to get everyone to start by writing down something positive about the topic and using this as a starting point.

It is the leader's task to watch the time during discussion and at a suitable point, leaving sufficient time before the end, stop the discussion and start summing up. This should normally include a summary of the main points and suggestions for action.

Leadership roles in different groups

The information above applies generally to most groups. There are some differences in the leadership behaviour required in different groups, however, and different styles may be appropriate in different situations. A leader who knows his or her own style is more likely to know how to make the most of personal strengths and limitations.

In exploratory or learning groups it is particularly important to be able to make and maintain good relationships. In this context the leader needs to be encouraging; to extend people's thinking; draw contributions together and build on from them, being patient while people work through their own thinking.

A group with a task requires firm leadership and a determination to achieve. This means keeping people to the point and making them work at the task.

A problem-solving group may need firm leadership to get everyone working at the task and requires a middle course between encouraging wide-ranging thinking and keeping people to the point. The leader's skill in drawing together points of agreement and finding a way forward is crucial.

A review group is one which meets regularly to deal with day-to-day business, for example, meetings of heads of department or heads of year. Leadership of review groups usually goes with a particular post or is elective and may thus be accepted without question, but initially the leader may have to work to persuade people to contribute. The leader of a review group must know the rules for running a formal meeting and the rules governing the status of the group: what it may and may not do or decide and what its responsibilities are.

A briefing group is one which meets for the dissemination of information. In some schools senior management or even the whole staff may meet for a short time daily for this purpose. Anyone running a briefing group needs skill in giving lucid and *expressed clearly* brief explanations in a way which is acceptable to the group.

Conclusion

The skills described in the various situations above are part of the same family of skills. The manager who learns to observe and interpret the behaviour of others, who develops skill in identifying the important points in any situation and where to go next, who has the skill to put something to another person in an acceptable way, has a set of skills for meeting most situations. A person can acquire these skills by observing others, by being self-critical and by analysing situations, as well as by formal training.

Chapter 13

Communication

The work of an organisation is only as good as its communication. Every school, even one which is very small, needs to give thought and care to communication both within the school and with the world outside. No school can ever afford to be complacent about the adequacy of its communication. Every organisation of any size has problems of communication from time to time and needs to work constantly to maintain communication if problems are not to multiply.

If two people are to understand each other, the words each one uses must mean approximately the same to them both. Yet each person's understanding of language is dependent upon his or her experience. For example, a parent whose own experience of education was entirely formal will have a different view of the process of teaching from that of a teacher who believes in a great deal of practical work and first-hand experience of many kinds. The parent's interpretation of the language they both use will be different from that of the teacher because of the differences in their frames of reference. We are currently seeing this kind of misunderstanding at national level between professional educators and politicians. Words used in common do not carry the same meaning for both parties.

Oral and written language are important modes of communication but in any piece of communication the message is conveyed not only by the content but also by the way it is presented, by the language chosen, the tone of voice and facial expression in the case of speech and by appearance in the case of written communication. These may modify or change the meaning of a message and the choice of language carries messages both about the speaker and about his or her view of those receiving the message. Where the words of a message conflict with the way it is conveyed there can be uncertainty and misunderstanding.

It is wise to use oral communication as a starting point, when anything disturbing, threatening or critical needs to be communicated. In emotional situations people tend to hear what they want to hear. If information is given orally, it is possible for them to ask questions and for the message to be repeated in different ways. This can then be followed up in writing. If information of this kind is initially given in writing, there is even more opportunity for misunderstanding and rumours can proliferate. It is also important to see how the listener is receiving a message which is critical or threatening and to react accordingly.

Written communication is produced and received in considerable quantities by most organisations and in most cases far more is produced than can be read. It is therefore valuable for those in senior posts to develop skill in skimming written material to decide which parts need to be read carefully, which need no more than a glance and which should be kept for reference. It is also important to write as economically as possible, arranging the text so that the eye catches what is important and so that there are few dense patches of text, which tend to put people off starting to read what is there.

The written word has certain advantages and disadvantages compared with the spoken word. It is, in a sense, permanent and this is both an advantage and a disadvantage. People can retain written communication and go over it at their own speed if they wish. The writer can go back over material and revise it until it seems to convey the message adequately. Word processing makes this easier and desk-top publishing allows a similar revision of layout and presentation. But writing is a more limited form of communication than speech, since it lacks the messages conveyed by movement, facial expression and tone of voice. Although written language conveys messages by format and choice of language, there are fewer clues from which to make inferences than there are in spoken language and since there is no opportunity to check that inferences are correct, the possibility of misunderstanding is greater.

All communication must be appropriate if it is to fulfil its purpose. This means it must match purpose, situation and audience or readership. It is particularly difficult to match language to the parent group because it is likely to contain people of widely differing backgrounds. It is important to avoid jargon, remembering that what seems to be perfectly normal language in school is read as jargon by those outside. It is also wise to avoid complex language.

Communication involves the following management tasks:

1 Ensure appropriate communication for everyone.
2 Create and maintain communication systems.
3 Ensure that information travels in all directions.
4 Seek feedback from all levels.
5 Evaluate the effectiveness of communication.

Ensure appropriate communication for everyone

The adults in the school

Adults in the school community include the headteacher, teaching staff, non-teaching staff and others, such as supply teachers and students who may be in the school for a period.

The lists given in Figures 13.1 to 13.7 are intended to provide both a summary of the information required by each group and a way of analysing the particular situation in a school. The 'source' column is intended to be completed, giving the way in which the particular information is conveyed, except where the source is obvious.

Information for teachers is normally provided through school handbooks of various kinds. If the school handbook is built up as a loose leaf document it makes it possible to add or change material as necessary. It needs to be reviewed and updated regularly and the process of producing papers for it and reviewing may be a valuable piece of staff development for a group.

Information is also needed by non-teaching staff. If they are made aware of the educational intentions of the school, they can often help to implement them.

The students

Students need to be given information about patterns and routines and rules of behaviour. Demands upon students need to be consistent as far as possible and each student needs to know where he or she fits into the pattern. Security comes from knowing what is and what is not allowed.

Information required	Source
Salary; conditions of service	Letter of appointment
Person to whom responsible	Job description
People for whom responsible	Job description
Tasks/duties for which responsible	Job description
Premises, equipment, materials for which responsible	Job description
Standards of work expected	Job description

Figure 13.1 Information needed by all adults in the school

They also need to be involved in some aspects of the planning and evaluation of the day-to-day life of the school. Real involvement in decision making is the best preparation for adult life in a democracy.

A school handbook for all students can be valuable in providing all the routine information such as details of any uniform, arrangements for meals, absence etc., together with annually updated information like a list of staff. This is likely to meet the needs of students more successfully if existing students are involved in some way in compiling it.

Students are likely to learn better if they see where what they are learning fits into the larger pattern. There is therefore a need to give them a good deal of information about the curriculum. The things they need to know are outlined in Figure 13.6. At later stages students will need to know the alternative courses available to them. They will also need information about out of school activities.

It is useful when considering any problem to think of what information is required in order to solve it. It can be helpful in sorting out an issue to make a flowchart and to add to each link the information which will be needed.

Written communication may pose problems of confidentiality. The school must decide what should be recorded in writing and who should have access to it.

Information required	Source
The school philosophy and policies	
The school development plan	
Information about school finances	
*Curriculum	
School patterns of responsibility	
Communication channels	
*Academic organisation	
Pastoral care organisation	
*Routines, e.g. lunch arrangements	
*Arrangements for students assessment	
Staff appraisal	
Staff development programme	
Normal contacts with parents	
*Information about individual students relevant for teaching/pastoral care	
Information about the governing body	
Normal contacts with other institutions and bodies	
Relevant LEA policies	
Services available from the LEA	

Figure 13.2 Information needed by teachers

Notes need to be made on various occasions. For example, it is wise to note important points made in discussions with parents and colleagues. It is also wise to make careful notes as soon as possible after the event of incidents which might escalate into cases for the courts and tribunals. An assault of any kind or a serious accident

Information required	Source
The overall aims of the school	
Ways in which they can contribute to the development/learning of the pupils	
Particular events in the school calendar of relevance to them	
Contribution to the overall life of the school expected from them	

Figure 13.3   Information needed by non-teaching staff

Information required	Source
Attendance of staff and students	
Behaviour of staff and students	
Effectiveness of organisation	
Effectiveness of teaching/learning	
State of buildings and environment	
State of equipment and materials	
Specific problems of organisation	
Specific problems of individual students	
Specific problems of individual staff	
Attitudes of staff, pupils and community	

Figure 13.4   Information needed by senior management

certainly requires this kind of treatment and any interview with a teacher or other member of staff which could lead to disciplinary action should be fully recorded. Interviews with a student which

Information required	Source
Routines for entering and leaving the school and rooms within it	
Routines for morning assembly, breaks, lunch times	
Overall organisation of the school	
The thinking and reasoning behind the school organisation	
The major responsibilities of the senior staff and teachers with whom the student comes in contact	
The names and responsibilities of non-teaching staff with whom a student may come in contact	
The timetable as it affects the individual student	
How students' work is assessed	
Arrangements for pastoral care	
The school's goals in training student behaviour	
Appropriate ways of dealing with routine matter, for example absence notes, the need for new stationery, lost property, arriving late	
The school rules – what is not allowed and why	

Figure 13.5 Information needed by students

might lead to suspension also need careful recording and this includes interviews with the student's parents.

Reports on teachers' work have now become more open than formerly, but confidential reports are still used in some contexts.

Information required	Source
The intended outcome of each piece of learning	
The criteria for the assessment of work	
The school marking system and the meaning of marks and grades	
The goals of each particular course of lessons, including what pupils should know and be able to do at the end of a given period	
The thinking behind any change of curriculum and the reasons for it	

Figure 13.6 Curriculum information needed by students

Whatever the system of reporting, a headteacher should normally make a teacher acquainted with any criticism of that teacher's work, so that if something critical is included in a report, it cannot be said that the criticism was unknown to the teacher.

It should also be remembered that one can no longer be certain that what is recorded in confidence will remain confidential. Those conducting enquiries and tribunals may legally demand to see information in confidential files and it is therefore even more important to be careful in recording and retaining material.

Create and maintain communication systems

The communication task facing the headteacher and senior staff of any school is both to see that the right information reaches the right people at the right time and to see that appropriate information reaches the management of the school. This needs to happen as efficiently as possible with the least possible effort on everyone's part.

In any organisation there are three parallel systems of communication:

1 *The formal system.* Every organisation needs systems to communicate plans and policies and everyday information. This requires definite official lines of communication which are as

Information required	Source
The school aims and philosophy	
Examination results	
Information about truancy	
School patterns of responsibility	
Communication channels	
Academic organisation	
Pastoral care organisation	
Discipline system and sanctions	
School rules	
Uniform regulations	
Homework patterns	
Arrangements for student assessment	
Normal contacts with parents	
What is expected of parents	
Arrangements for meeting staff to discuss children's progress	
Other meetings for parents	
Opportunities for parents to contribute to the school	
Lunch arrangements	
Information about the governing body	

Figure 13.7 Information needed by parents

short and direct as possible and which define clearly the responsibility of different members of staff for communicating information to others.

2 *The informal system.* The informal system is frequently more rapid than the formal one but less accurate and is often concerned with communication which is threatening or alarming. This needs to be taken into account when planning formal communication. For example, important information which could be misinterpreted should be given to everyone authoritatively, quickly, clearly and fully, so that it is difficult for the informal system to misinterpret it. The informal system is also useful in complementing the formal system.

3 *The inferential system.* Every activity of people within an organisation is a form of communication. Inferences are made from a person's tone of voice, appearance, movement, choice of language, matters selected for comment, the arrangement of the environment and much else besides. There is sometimes a gap between what a school or a person thinks is being communicated and the message actually being received. For example, a school may be keen to foster very good relationships with parents and other visitors to the school, but be unaware that people entering the school are made to feel unwelcome by the lack of indication of where to go and the attitude of the receptionist.

Effective communication

No communication system ensures that people actually absorb what is offered to them. It is therefore important to consider what makes people receptive. They are most likely to take in communication when:

– it is personal, i.e. addressed to them
– it fulfils a need or rouses an interest:
   • communication about anything significant to an individual will be absorbed. For example, very few people miss information about salaries or condition of service. A strong interest can sometimes be used as a lead in to other information.
– it is seen to give power or status:
   • people tend to absorb information which comes to them because of the office they hold or if it enables them to know something which others would like to know.

- the communication requires action:
  - most people hate to let others down. If a communication demands action which is in public, in that it can be seen to be done, it is usually absorbed.
- they identify with the organisation:
  - people will take in communication when they care about the organisation from which it comes and their jobs within it.
- the presentation is right
- the source is respected:
  - the person who gives a message affects whether it is taken in or not. Most headteachers will recall times when someone has said 'You tell them because they'll listen to you'. The status and personal standing of the person communicating is important.
- the context predisposes the listener to be receptive:
  - communication is best when all the conditions are good. It is easy to be distracted from a communication by discomfort – for example, uncomfortable seats at a meeting or illegible writing. A frequent distraction is that of receiving too many pieces of communication at once!

Things which go wrong

There are many things which go wrong with communication. They may go wrong because of faults in the system. A communication system for passing information through the school depends upon each person in the chain taking part. A system which depends upon heads of department both passing on and collecting information from their members falls down if some departments decide that they do not need meetings or a head of department decides not to take part or even if the head of department is absent and no substitute has been appointed for communication.

A communication system which demands a radical change from the past will be difficult to work initially not only because people may not play their parts adequately but also because the informal system which complements the formal system also needs to find a new way of working. It is often better to look at the way in which communication is currently working and look for developments which improve this than to go for a completely new system.

Things will go wrong if no one checks occasionally that the system works. This does not mean insisting that there is only one way of operating, but if, for example, the system depends upon certain people passing on certain kinds of messages, they will tend to do this less carefully as time passes and as pressures increase and may need occasional reminders of their responsibilities.

Schools are rarely generously staffed with clerical assistance and any communication which relies too heavily upon typed papers may founder because the clerical staff cannot keep up with what is being demanded.

Things go wrong because of the presentation of communication. Unless they are very strongly motivated busy people are prepared to make only a small amount of effort to understand something which isn't clear.

There is an art in giving people exactly the amount of information they can manage. Too much type on a page and a person does not start to read it but sets it aside to read later – but later never comes. Too much talk and people switch off. On the other hand a person given only half a message may invent the other half incorrectly. Somewhere there is an optimum for all messages. It is worth looking at how the advertising world gets messages across effectively.

Things go wrong with communication because people are as they are. Messages may be interpreted in the light of previous experience of which the sender is unaware. They may be misunderstood intentionally or unintentionally. Mr Smith may so dislike Miss Jones that he cannot hear what she is saying. A message may be distorted by the status of its sender, receiving additional attention if the sender is very senior and being ignored if the sender is very junior.

Ensure that information travels in all directions

It is very easy for a headteacher to feel that when there is a good top-down communication, this is sufficient. Or he or she may feel that everything possible is being done to get views back from people but somehow not very much comes back.

If this is the case, several things may be happening. People may be discouraged from putting forward their ideas because the headteacher is known to have so many. It is a problem for a person who is full of ideas to hold back sometimes in order to persuade other people to voice their ideas, creating an atmosphere in which people feel able to make suggestions.

Another possibility is that ideas brought to the headteacher may appear not to be welcomed or even recognised when they are advanced very tentatively. Headteachers and teachers who complain that their staff or their students have few ideas may be dismissing those which are advanced without realising they are doing so, often by sounding lukewarm, or talking too much when they should listen and draw out, or by missing ideas altogether.

A headteacher can help to ensure that information travels upwards by creating situations in which staff views must be put forward. Working parties and study groups dealing with some aspect of school life provide opportunities for people to start suggesting ideas. Questionnaires or requests to years or departments for views and ideas will also serve this purpose, as will opportunities for people to discuss an issue at length at a staff conference.

It is often difficult to get information to travel sideways in a secondary school, particularly if the departmental organisation is strong. The development of faculties should help this but the barriers may then be between faculties instead of departments. It can help if opportunities are provided for discussion about cross-curricular learning, such as work on study skills or problem solving, asking each department to give information about its contribution, leading people towards a general plan for such areas of work. Discussion about school finances may also provide this kind of opportunity for people to be aware of what others are doing.

Sideways communication is also developed when individuals and groups are encouraged to consult each other. The senior staff of a school are often in a strong position to foster cooperation because they can see where people are pursuing similar ends. School events, such as plays or field study, may also encourage people in different departments to work together and thus get into the habit of communicating with each other.

Seek feedback from all levels

It is easy in the busy round of daily life in a school for a head-teacher to go weeks without talking to some members of staff. It is important to talk in depth not only with senior staff but also with the youngest and most junior members of staff and with students at different levels, listening to what they say and asking questions in order to find out. An after-lunch coffee with a different group of staff one week and students the next, will enable a headteacher over the course of a year to hear from a large number of people. It is wise not to mix the groups too much in doing this. Young teachers are more likely to talk freely with other young teachers present than with people who are senior in age and experience. Likewise students from the intake year are more likely to talk freely in a group with their contemporaries than in a mixed group.

A headteacher may also get this kind of information informally from frequent walking round the school and from being in the staffroom from time to time, but a headteacher who relies on this as the main source should check occasionally whether the informal discussion covers a full range of people. It is very easy to converse a lot with the talkative and extrovert and to miss the quieter people who do not put themselves forward. The ancillary staff also need to be included in discussion from time to time, so that their point of view is heard.

Any headteacher or senior member of staff gets a filtered view of what people think. People tell the headteacher what they want him or her to know, which may not be the same as what the headteacher wants to know. It is necessary to work continually to get behind this.

Evaluate the effectiveness of communication

The analysis given for assessing the different communication requirements earlier in this chapter is a useful evaluation tool for the system. The area which has not been considered is the loading on different people. In any school there are some people who are buried under the communications they receive and others who continually complain that no one tells them anything. It is useful occasionally to assess who is receiving which communications and where the pressures are most likely to be.

One way of checking the communication system is to ask questions against a definition of a good system. In a good system:
– the right messages get to the right people at the right time. Check by asking:
  • How often do people complain of not getting information?
  • How often do people fail to act on information which was believed to be sent?
  • How often does the wrong message go over?

- there are clearly understood channels of communication upwards, downwards and sideways and these are all used. Check by asking:
  - How much information do the headteacher and senior staff actually receive which has come upwards?
  - If people are asked how they communicate or receive communication, is the answer the expected one?
  - Does communication actually appear to come through the channels planned?
- everyone feels well informed, but not overwhelmed, by communication and people at every level appear to feel involved and conscious of participation. Check by asking:
  - Does anyone complain of getting too much or too little communication?
  - Are there any major gaps in communication?
- communication takes the minimum time for its proper working. Check by asking:
  - Does any part of the system take a lot of time?
  - Is what is communicated really necessary?
  - Does all the paper which crosses the desks of the senior management team really need to come to them?
  - Are meetings well planned and led and felt to be worth the time spent on them?
  - Are appropriate modes of communication being used?
  - Is the optimum use being made of information technology?
- an overview of the system is maintained and practice is regularly reviewed. Check by asking:
  - Is there an adequate overview?
  - Should more be done to review the system?
- the inferential system gives the same messages as the formal system. Check by asking:
  - What views about the overall aims of the school are being put over officially to staff, parents and students?
  - What is actually being communicated?
  - Is anything happening which is counter to the official view?

Chapter 14

Staff selection and development

Staff selection and staff development are two aspects of the same process. A school looks for a person with certain skills and qualities in making an appointment. After appointment it is the task of the head and senior staff to enable the person concerned to develop in ways which enhance his or her ability to undertake a new role, building on from previous experience and using appraisal as a means of identifying emerging needs.

Staff development is wider than this, however. A school needs to have a professional development plan to enable staff to meet the demands of the school development plan which will include the many demands coming from the National Curriculum and other national initiatives.

The management tasks involved in staff selection and development are as follows:

1 Organise and assist with staff appointments.
2 Establish a policy for staff development and appraisal.
3 Create a development programme for all staff.
4 Evaluate the staff development programme.
5 Maintain staff records and provide any necessary reports.

Organise and assist with staff appointments

Although the responsibility for staff appointments has now been transferred from the LEA to governors, the number of people involved in the appointment of staff may make the headteacher's role a complex one. The Post Project report on the appointment of secondary school headteachers (Morgan *et al.* 1983) described the effect of the then system of appointing secondary school headteachers as placing far more emphasis on qualities of personality, which are not easy to assess in interview, than on the skills needed to do the job. Too little emphasis was given, the authors felt, to the ability to undertake the management tasks of headship.

Although this study is now over ten years old, much that it says will still be true. The authors point out that very few of those involved in interviewing have been trained as assessors and that, since the questioning is often given little preparation, what is discovered in the course of an interview may not give the interviewing panel an adequate idea of the suitability of the candidate for the post. They suggest that other ways of assessing candidates might offer more information than interviewing alone, which is known to be an uncertain way of assessing people.

Schools are now in a much stronger position to set up staff selection procedures than they were formerly and headteachers need to persuade their governors to allow a more in-depth method of appointing staff than a single interview, especially for appointment to more senior posts.

The task of matching person to post involves collecting all the evidence available about the candidate and at the same time offering the candidate evidence about the nature of the school and the kind of philosophy which the headteacher and senior staff try to foster. The governors have to decide whether a particular candidate matches the post under consideration and the candidate has to decide whether this is the school for him or her. The evidence on which these decisions are made is gradually revealed during the process of appointment. It is one of the most important tasks which any governing body undertakes.

Before an appointment can be made, the job description should be brought up to date and a candidate description drawn up describing the kind of person wanted to fill a particular vacancy. It should contain statements of what is required by way of:

- qualifications, knowledge, skills, abilities
- experience
- special aptitudes and qualities
- particular interests

Information about these points should be given in the further particulars of the post and the list made available to those making the appointment. The further particulars should give enough information to prevent people wasting their time applying for posts for which they are clearly unsuited. The ideal advertisement and further particulars should attract the right candidates only.

Some schools may now be in a position to develop their own application forms. It is important to have an application form because in a letter of application candidates can more easily disguise the information they offer than when a form is used. The application form should include space for a letter or statement in support of the application which gives information about the way in which the candidate's particular experience and qualifications fit him or her for the post in question. This kind of information is more likely to be forthcoming if some advice is given about the statement required, preferably on the form itself, but otherwise in the further particulars.

Once the applications have been received, they need to be sifted to decide which are sufficiently interesting to warrant seeking further information. This needs to be done even when there are very few applications, since it is a waste of everyone's time to pursue candidates who are clearly unsuitable.

At this stage a headteacher may wish to ask for confidential information about a number of the candidates. This should add to the information available and is more likely to do so if specific questions are asked. A particularly useful question is 'Would you appoint this candidate to a similar post in your school?' and it is also useful to ask for strengths and weaknesses. It is wise to get more than one report on a candidate, particularly for a senior post and it is unwise to make any appointment without written information of this kind, although pressure of time may sometimes make this necessary. Interviewing is known to be fallible and even the most experienced interviewer makes mistakes.

The governors may or may not wish to be involved in making the short list. Even if they are prepared to delegate the task to the headteacher, it is wise to involve other people. However good a person's judgement, mistakes are less likely when more than one person is involved. Most appointments at other than deputy headship level should involve other members of staff who will have to work with the person appointed and they will therefore need to be consulted at all stages.

An analysis of some kind is useful in studying application forms and it is helpful to draw up a pro forma which sets out the qualifications and experience so that they can be compared.

The time the candidates are in school should be carefully planned. Every part of the day is an opportunity for getting information from them and giving them information and even when interviews are taking place, it is a waste of opportunity to leave candidates sitting doing nothing. Such time might be used for parallel sets of interviews or for discussion with other staff. In addition to the formal interviews it should be possible to provide the following opportunities:

1 A tour of the buildings, particularly the rooms in which the successful candidate will work and the staff facilities. They need to get an honest picture, with difficulties and problems made plain, so that they know what they might be coming to.
2 Time to talk at some length with those who will work most closely with the selected candidate. This can be in a social context over lunch or coffee, but there is a good deal to be said for some preliminary planning of topics to be discussed so that necessary ground can be covered.
3 Some social time with members of staff. Although it has to be accepted that all the time the candidates are in school has some relevance for selection, the social parts of the day can be more relaxed and in practice offer a rather different kind of information to the selector.
4 Time to ask questions of the headteacher so that they are clear about the nature of the post they might be accepting.

The actual selection process should be designed to elicit as much relevant information as possible from each candidate in such a way that they can be compared.

The education service tends to limit selection procedures to interviewing, but there is no reason why other ways of selecting should not be employed. For example, each candidate might be asked to teach a small group for a short period of time. or where the school is seeking someone in a management post, each candidate might be asked to chair a short discussion on some topic involving all the candidates. This will both elicit information from everyone and also give information about the skill of the group chairperson. Some useful information is given in *A Handbook on Selecting Senior Staff for Schools* (Morgan *et al.* 1984).

Whatever selection procedures are used, it is important that an interview is included. This is the only way of getting some of the necessary information and it also gives governors the opportunity to play their part. If possible there should be more than one set of concurrent interviews with small groups of interviewers looking for particular things. This means that each candidate is interviewed for longer and there is therefore more information available on which to make a decision. If the governors are not happy to do this, it may be possible to have preliminary interviews followed by a more formal interview with governors. Governors should, if possible, be persuaded against interviewing in a large body. This does not allow for questions to be pursued and tends to put candidates off.

The governors need to know in advance all the details of the person required and the way in which the evidence is being built up. In particular the headteacher needs to explain plans for questioning and ask governors if they would be willing to explore particular areas of questioning, remembering that the governing body may well include some people who are practised interviewers able to contribute a lot and will need little guidance. Others who are less experienced may be glad to be asked to do something specific and may have a useful contribution to make because they come fresh to the procedure.

In questioning it is helpful to remember that a useful guide to candidates' ability is in what they can tell the panel about what they have actually done, providing that it is followed up with probing questions to establish that the experience is genuine. Most questions should be followed up with others which probe so that there is a check on what people say.

In selection interviewing as in short-listing, people have to guard against their own prejudices and reactions. It is, of course, important that a headteacher sees that the person chosen is someone with whom he or she can work, but it is easy to be drawn to an exciting candidate and turn aside a less exciting person who could actually bring far more to the job. Interviewers should know their own temptations and weaknesses.

At the end of the day a decision has to be made in the light of all the evidence available. The chairperson may have personal ideas about the best way to arrive at a decision, but the following pattern is useful:

1 Check that everyone is aware of all the evidence, perhaps by getting someone to sum up and then ask each member of the interviewing panel to list the candidates in order of preference, using any gradings made to help with this.

2 Ask everyone to state the candidates they would put at the bottom of the list. This usually narrows the field and avoids wasting time discussing unlikely candidates.

3 Ask everyone for their first, second and third choice, if there are that many candidates. This narrows the field and concentrates attention on a small number of names. It may even provide the final decision.

4 Review the evidence about the names left in and discuss them further. This will usually produce the final decision.

If the candidates are still waiting, the successful candidate should be offered the post. Any statements made to the successful candidate about salary or responsibilities at this stage may be regarded as legally binding so it is important that prior decisions have been reached about these points and that any information given is correct. The unsuccessful candidates should be thanked for coming and if possible some feedback on performance should be given to them, perhaps sharing out this task so that each person has a chance to talk with a member of the appointing panel.

All the information from the interview should be kept for a period in case queries arise. The papers of the successful candidate become the starting point for the personal file, giving information on which further professional development can be based.

The proof of the effectiveness of any selection process is not only in the quality of the staff built up over time, but also in the extent to which the people appointed turn out to give surprises, both good and bad. In the ideal situation a selector should have a good idea at the end of the day of the kind of person who has been appointed. It is useful to review interview notes after six months or so to see how far the picture formed at the interview was an accurate one.

Establish a policy for staff development and appraisal

The headteacher and senior staff of a school are responsible for seeing that their colleagues have the opportunity and encouragement to develop in their work. This is normally taken to apply to teaching staff, but there is also a case for considering the development of other staff if development is regarded as important for work in the current post and not simply as preparation for the future.

Poster and Poster, in discussing appraisal, suggest that it can be seen from two different points of view (Poster and Poster 1991). These two points of view are also relevant for professional development generally. We can ask what the aims of the school are and plan for the development of staff so that these aims can be achieved. Or we can look at the needs of individuals and help them plan first to be effective in their current posts and then to learn in preparation for possible promotion.

The learning needs of teachers

Teachers enter the profession with a body of skills and knowledge from training and the beginnings of teaching skills. Schools are playing an increasing part in the training of teachers and the school in which a teacher starts work is probably the most important single source of learning from then on and likely to affect the way that teacher learns for many years, perhaps throughout his or her teaching life. This is so whether or not the headteacher and staff make a conscious effort to help new teachers to develop. Newly qualified teachers are impressionable at the beginning of their careers and the examples they are shown and the training they receive from colleagues are important. It is in the context of actually doing the job that skills are developed and knowledge acquired and consolidated.

Teachers learn through interaction with their professional environment. They form and develop a frame of reference by which they judge their own professional activity and that of others. They acquire new knowledge and develop the skills to meet the tasks and situations they encounter. Oldroyd and Hall note that:

> institutions identified for their good staff development programmes tend to exhibit a collegial, participative style of leadership where senior staff work as a team and are ready to:
> - consult staff about needs and priorities
> - delegate significant responsibilities
> - encourage staff ownership of INSET policies and programmes
> - invite open review of processes and activities
> - identify and use talented staff to lead INSET activities
> - network good practice between groups within the institution
> - lead by example, by themselves engaging in their own professional development

- contribute towards a positive climate by offering professional support and personal counselling to staff.

(Olroyd and Hall 1988)

Knowledge and skill may be developed in a variety of ways. Teachers may read, selecting books which offer what they want. They may question colleagues, watch them at work, listen to what they say, trying an idea here, a method or a style there, gradually evolving their personal teaching style. The school may offer opportunities for working with other teachers to particular ends, perhaps seeking the solution to a problem or making plans for a piece of work or planning an in-service day. In the secondary school, much of this development happens within the subject department. Appraisal should also contribute to teacher development.

Teachers also have opportunities outside the school. They may listen to the radio and watch television programmes which seem to offer something useful. They select from in-service programmes on offer. They may also take part in inter-school activities.

Many schools now feel that some of the best in-service work comes from their own in-service programmes when these are planned to meet the needs of the school and the teachers and involve staff in their planning.

In all these learning situations teachers will be constantly taking in and sorting out new materials and ideas in their minds, fitting them into their emerging frames of reference, digesting them and making them peculiarly their own. Alongside this, new teachers will be developing in maturity and this too affects their work in school.

All schools need a professional development policy. This might include statements about the following:

- overall philosophy and attitudes
- the people whom the policy concerns (non-teaching as well as teaching staff)
- the possible professional development activities
- the organisation and responsibilities for professional development
- the way needs will be assessed
- the part played by appraisal
- provision for induction and for newly qualified teachers
- provision for management training
- the way in which provision for individuals will be built up
- the way in which teachers' progress and development will be recorded

Organisation

The responsibility for the professional development of staff is now very much with the individual school, this means that each school needs an organisation that can provide for this. Professional development needs to be the responsibility of a senior member of staff with support from a representative committee of teachers which meets regularly and which holds occasional meetings with other staff to discuss the development programme. The professional development committee should be responsible for identifying needs both for the school as a whole and for individuals, and for planning and implementing the overall staff development programme.

The staff development programme needs to be linked clearly with the school development programme so that any training needed to implement the school development plan is clearly identified in the staff development programme. The plan should take into account the need:

– for particular development and knowledge within the school at the present time
– to prepare for future needs
– to keep staff stimulated by the work
– to keep everyone up to date with what is happening professionally outside the school.

Preparation for future needs is partly a matter of looking two or three years ahead and, as far as is possible, anticipating the needs that will exist then. It is not customary for schools to plan for succession in the same way as in some industrial concerns, but it is nevertheless a good idea to ensure that enough people are acquiring the managerial skills which will be needed to succeed those in middle and senior management, so that there is a choice of people from within the school to set alongside candidates from outside when filling future vacancies.

A school not only needs formal plans for staff development which require assessment of the overall needs of the school and of individuals within it, and the creation and development of a programme. It also needs to use informal opportunities which arise as means to these ends. This requires clear thinking about direction and goals.

The emphasis in staff development will vary according to the particular emphasis at any given time and the particular group of staff in office. There are, nevertheless, some staff development activities which should be a permanent part of any programme, although the way they are conducted may change.

Induction New staff, however experienced in the work, need induction into the particular school organisation and systems. This should involve meetings which explain school policies and systems; induction into the role of form teacher where appropriate; information on students; briefing on relevant work already undertaken by staff; arrangements for support for new members of staff by someone experienced in the school and some arrangement for checking by senior management that they are settling in happily and for dealing with any problems.

Provision for newly qualified staff The probationary year has now been abolished but the need to support and continue the training of newly qualified teachers, including licensed and articled teachers, remains. They will not only need the induction programme but also support and further training in their work in the classroom and there should be a clear responsibility for providing this. Most newly qualified teachers need reassurance that they are making progress and should have opportunities to see other teachers at work as well as being seen in the classroom fairly frequently themselves. They also need good opportunities for discussing their work with more experienced teachers. This is in the first place a responsibility for heads of department, but there is a need for another person with overall responsibility for supporting the newly qualified and those in the process of becoming qualified.

Opportunities for all teachers to reflect on performance, work on classroom skills and management development All teachers improve their work by reflecting on it. The trouble is that schools are extremely busy places where time for reflection is hard to find. The senior management of the school needs to see that the organisation is such that they themselves make time to reflect and that they also create time and opportunity and give encouragement for others to reflect. This is most likely to happen when a group of people come together to discuss their work and one way of providing this is to use a staff development day occasionally for this kind of reflection.

There is a sense in which we create reflection opportunities by giving people more rather than less to do. The department asked to make a statement justifying its demands for a larger part of the financial cake or explaining, for the school prospectus, the reasons for teaching its subject, will somehow find time to do this because it really matters. In the process department members will do some thinking about their work which they might not otherwise have done. One task of management is to stimulate and structure thinking by asking questions and making demands.

Reflection on performance is further created by teachers seeing others at work. The headteacher and senior staff, including heads of department, have a role here, but there is also value in peer-group evaluation. If two or more teachers can come together and organise themselves so that they see something of each other's attempts to achieve particular targets in the classroom, this too is valuable.

Appraisal

Schools are now required to appraise all teachers. This is an idea which has gradually been gaining adherents and which schools are now putting into practice. The pilot studies of appraisal suggested that it was easier to introduce it in a situation where there is regular reviewing of the work of the school.

It must be remembered that some teachers may see appraisal as threatening. Wragg notes that 'the fear of a humiliation ritual is one that bedevils the act of appraisal wherever it takes place' and 'the act of appraisal can force people to confront themselves in ways they would normally wish to avoid' (Wragg 1987). These problems need to be kept in mind in running an appraisal system.

The purposes of appraisal need to be clear to everyone involved. The Secretary of State's letter to Chief Education Officers states that appraisal schemes shall be designed to:

- help teachers to identify ways of enhancing their professional skill
- assist in planning the in-service training and professional development of teachers individually and collectively
- help individual teachers, their headteachers, governing body and local education authorities (where appropriate) to see where a new or modified assignment would help the professional development of individual teachers and improve their career prospects

- identify the potential of teachers for career development with the aim of helping them, where possible, through appropriate in-service training
- provide help to teachers having difficulties with their performance, through appropriate guidance, counselling and training. Disciplinary and dismissal procedures shall remain quite separate but may need to draw on relevant information from appraisal records
- inform those responsible for providing references for teachers
- enhance the overall management of schools.

(DES 1990)

Dean adds to this list:

- to provide a means of coordinating the work of the department and the school
- to provide help and support for teachers in a management role
- to support teachers with management roles in their responsibility for the work of their colleagues
- as an opportunity for praising what is good and dealing with unsatisfactory elements in a teacher's work
- to provide the teacher with an opportunity to ensure that others know about his or her work and to give an opportunity for expressing views
- to provide the appraiser with additional knowledge about what is happening and to enable him or her to have a view of the department or the school as a whole
- to provide an opportunity for those in leadership roles to influence the thinking of others and be influenced by their views.

(Dean 1991)

Sources of information for appraisal might include the following:

1 Self-assessment by the teacher concerned.
2 Planned observation of the teacher's work in the classroom.
3 Test and examination results.
4 Study of students' work.
5 Information from students.
6 Observation of the teacher in a pastoral role.
7 Observation of the teacher in a management role.
8 Other observations.

Appraisal requires observation of the person being appraised in his or her working environment. This requires the establishment of criteria which should be worked out and agreed by the whole staff. It requires some thought about what constitutes good teaching, what constitutes effective behaviour in a management role and what should be included about other aspects of a teacher's work, such as pastoral care.

The plan for observation of the teacher's work should include, if possible, some opportunity for self-evaluation and there are many published forms for doing this and for classroom observation (Suffolk LEA 1987; Dean 1991). There are also many LEA lists. However, there is also value in schools making their own lists which can be drawn up to match their particular aims and objectives.

There will need to be agreement about the pattern of lessons to be observed. The appraiser also needs to establish, before observing a lesson, what the teacher is trying to achieve. There needs to be agreement among staff as to the form the observation will take, whether everyone should use similar criteria for observation, what they should be and how they should be recorded. It is also important for discussion of the lesson to take place as soon as possible after the observation while what happened is fresh in the minds of observer and teacher.

Appraisal interviewing is an important skill and if this task is to be done adequately, at least an hour needs to be set aside for each person, if there is to be sufficient time to explore thinking in some detail.

Both interviewer and interviewee need to prepare for the appraisal interview. Classroom and other observation is only part of the necessary preparation. It is helpful if the appraisee provides some form of self-evaluation in writing before the interview. This might state objectives, success in achieving them and particular problems and difficulties. The appraiser needs to study any relevant background information, including the previous appraisal documents and notes of any discussions which have taken place since the last appraisal.

The appraisal interview is an opportunity for interviewer and interviewee to plan together. The idea is to review the immediate past, look at the current situation and agree goals for the future. It may provide an opportunity to speak frankly about areas of work where improvement is required, but this should be in the context of mutual planning for overall improvement and should be positive and supportive as far as possible. It should also be an occasion for praise and encouragement. If the interview is done well and positively it can be a powerful means of development for individuals and a valuable way for the management of the school to gain an overall picture of how people see the school, their colleagues, their work and themselves.

The need to train appraisers will continue as new people are appointed to management roles and it must be the responsibility of the school to see that training takes place before people are expected to appraise others.

Each school has to decide who should appraise whom. The DES circular (July 1991) made it clear that it was expected that teachers would be appraised by a senior colleague. The most obvious arrangement is that each line manager should interview those staff for whom he or she is responsible. This would seem to be the desirable state since each line manager should be responsible for the development of his or her staff. This is not always straightforward, however. There are also situations in which people work in more than one department and where senior staff do some teaching in a department. Responsibility for pastoral care also takes most staff into a second set of responsibilities. The DES circular suggests that each appraiser should, in most circumstances, appraise no more than four people, but there are some departments with more than four people. There are also situations where line managers are not competent and their staff are unhappy about them as appraisers. Some schools are dealing with these problems by allowing teachers the choice of appraiser. This has the advantage that teachers have confidence in their appraiser but it can happen that the appraiser is not competent to appraise teaching in the teacher's subject. This could be overcome by asking a subject specialist to observe teaching and using his or her report as part of the data collected for the appraisal. Another way of dealing with this is to ask all staff to note, in confidence, those people on a list of appraisers whom they would not want to appraise them. It then becomes possible to allocate staff to appraisers taking this into account. It is also important to see that appraisers whose skill teachers appear to doubt are sufficiently trained. Appraisers also have the task of getting information from colleagues about each appraisee's ability in pastoral work and other activities.

Create a development programme for all staff

The professional development programme must cover all aspects of the life and work of the school. We can start by considering what teachers need to learn. Much of this learning will start during training but the school enables it to continue developing.

Personal development

Teachers' personalities and their personal qualities are crucial factors in teaching success. Most people learn better when they like and respect the teacher. A teacher who is a mature human being offers a model to young people which may, in important ways, affect their attitudes to school, to learning and to the world.

All teachers are still developing as people. The treatment they receive from those senior to them, the extent to which their views are considered and treated with respect, the attitudes shown to them, all affect their development.

Child development

Teachers need knowledge of the normal patterns of physical, intellectual, emotional and social development of children if they are to understand those they teach and recognise deviations from the norm. They may have to deal with issues outside their own upbringing and personal experience such as drug-taking, alcoholism, violence, HIV and AIDS and family breakdown. There needs to be an awareness in the school of these issues and some agreement about the best way to deal with them. Teachers need the support of colleagues so that they, in turn, can support young people in difficulties.

Knowledge of learning and teaching

Teachers tend to be more effective when they have adequate theoretical backing for what they do and can use their theoretical knowledge to improve their practice. They also need a range of teaching methods and learning strategies so that they can select appropriately for different teaching situations.

Group behaviour

Teaching in school depends upon teachers' ability to manage children and young people in groups. The skill with which an experienced teacher manages groups of students normally reflects an understanding of the way groups work, even if this is not consciously acquired knowledge. Knowledge of the way groups control individuals and an ability to recognise the effects of both competition and cooperation are valuable to all teachers.

Teachers need the following skills:

- ability to observe students, recognising the needs and progress of each
- ability to communicate through exposition, questioning, leading discussion and so on
- skill in organising and planning
- ability to evaluate their own work and that of students.

At a more senior level teachers need not only the skills of the classroom teacher but also management skills, including the following:

- the ability to make good relationships with adults and the inter-personal skills involved in working with them
- skill in eliciting ideas from colleagues and drawing them together
- skill in identifying aims and objectives, making them explicit, planning and organising so as to achieve them
- the ability to analyse and solve problems
- skill in handling the various administrative tasks of senior management.

Those in ancillary posts may also have learning needs. These may be more difficult to define than those of teachers, but they still need to be considered.

There are three main ways in which learning takes place for all staff in schools.

They learn as part of their work

Teachers learn by studying their own work through:

- opportunities to talk over work with more experienced colleagues
- provision of feedback on performance for a single lesson or work over a period of time, perhaps as part of the appraisal process

- use of self-assessment techniques such as check lists
- feedback from students

They learn from other teachers through:

- formal and informal staffroom discussion
- observing students with other teachers
- observing other teachers at work
- visiting other schools
- being involved with other teachers in experimental and problem-solving activities
- being involved with other teachers in evaluation and assessment
- action research in which a group of teachers together studies methods of improving some aspect of their work
- coaching in particular skills identified through classroom observation
- experimental work in the classroom
- shadowing a student for a day
- shadowing a senior colleague
- appraisal meetings

They are involved in opportunities for acquiring management skills, which may include:

- participation in decision making activities
- being given opportunity to exercise responsibility
- being given opportunity to exercise inter-personal skills with adults
- understudying a particular post for a period as part of a staff development programme

They learn by specific provision within the school

Schools now normally provide formal opportunities for staff development, which may include:

- provision of specific written material and discussion about it
- involvement in the preparation of written material such as a staff handbook or scheme of work
- staff conferences
- seminars or discussions on a regular basis
- job enrichment opportunities – perhaps being given additional responsibility
- job exchange

- use of prepared materials with a staff group, for example, pre-pared in-service packages, videos
- viewing of television programmes made for discussion by teachers
- joint visits to other schools or centres by groups of teachers
- specific encouragement to undertake relevant professional reading, perhaps by requesting teachers to read a particular book and report on it to colleagues

They learn through external provision

However good the internal programme, it is important for teachers to go out and meet teachers from other places. The cost of this to schools means that such opportunities need to be very carefully chosen. In-service opportunities of this kind should service the needs of the school as well as those of the individual teacher.

Opportunity to take part in inter-school discussions and work-ing parties may not be labelled in-service or even be thought of as having a professional development purpose, but nevertheless may make a contribution to the development of those taking part. This kind of opportunity is particularly valuable to teachers who have been a long time in post but who feel that the in-service courses on offer are unlikely to contribute much to their development.

Evaluate the staff development programme

The provision for staff development should be evaluated regularly. Each part of the programme should include some evaluation and the whole programme should be evaluated at intervals. This is a task for the staff development committee. There are a number of distinct methods of evaluating which include the following:

- questionnaires
- other documentary evidence
- discussion with those who have experienced the programme
- interviewing a sample of individuals
- observation of whether suitable programmes have had an effect
- evidence from students
- value-for-money assessment

The following questions may be useful in evaluating the programme:

1 Have we a satisfactory staff development policy and programme? How widespread is its application?
2 Have we an adequate method of assessing needs? Are we missing any which are important?
3 What opportunities do we offer teachers to improve their teaching skills?
4 To what extent do teachers work together sharing problems,
   experience and skills?
5 What opportunities are there for teachers to acquire and
   develop management skills?
6 What opportunities are we offering to heads of department,
   heads of year and other equivalent posts?
7 What are we gaining from our appraisal programme?
8 Are we getting value for money in what we spend on our own
   programme?
9 Are we getting value for money in what we spend on sending
   people on courses?

Maintain staff records and provide any necessary reports

It is the responsibility of management to see that an adequate
record is kept on each individual member of staff. These records
should include information about the work which teachers have
done during their time in the school and this will form the basis of
any report written on members of staff who are candidates for
promotion or who are failing.

One way of providing this information is to get teachers
annually to write a note of the work done during the year, including both curricular and extra-curricular activities. This can then go
into the file exactly as the teacher wrote it. This is slightly different
from the kind of information which needs to be provided for
appraisal which should have more of a self-evaluation element.

All headteachers find themselves asked to provide reports on
the work of teachers who are candidates for promotion. A headteacher may receive a request which lists questions to be answered,
but many such requests are more general. Information about the
teacher's experience in the previous years may be helpful in this
context. It is wise to give the teacher concerned some idea of what
is being said. If this involves actually showing the reference to the
teacher a note about this should be included.

Teachers should be able to see their own files upon request.

Chapter 15

School and community

Schools do not exist in isolation. They are part of a wider community within the neighbourhood and nationally. They are also part of a professional community of those schools which contribute students to them and of the colleges and other institutions to which students may go. Recent developments have stressed the need for schools to make relationships, not only with parents, but also with employers and the neighbourhood community. This poses problems in the use of time, because the central role of the school lies in teaching students, but external relationships need to be cultivated for the overall benefit of the students and for the future development of the school.

The headteacher of a school is in a particular relationship to the world outside the school. He or she stands on the boundary and has the task of creating and maintaining many of the outside relationships. The headteacher is the official representative of the school and must endeavour to see that the school is represented to the outside world. It is also important to see that the school is using all the possible contributions it can from people outside it and at the same time is trying to protect the staff from some of the pressures.

There is now a strong emphasis on meeting the needs of the school's clients, the parents and students. The school which does not succeed in carrying local parents with it will dwindle in numbers and consequently in resources. This is a much more complex issue than some would have us believe, however. The clients of a school are likely to have a wide range of frames of reference and the school which makes carrying parents with it the only criterion for its ways of working is likely to be in difficulty. The school needs a philosophy and a sense of direction which is agreed with its governors and as far as possible with its parents, so that parents choose the school because they believe it has a philosophy they can accept. In relation to the community, management has five key responsibilities:

1 Represent the school to the world outside.
2 Support governors in developing their work.
3 Involve parents where appropriate.
4 Establish relationships with employers.
5 Encourage the use of the community for learning.

Represent the school to the world outside

The headteacher, as representative of the school to the world outside, will undoubtedly need to attend various meetings on behalf of the school in situations where delegation is not possible. This activity is not only interesting but may very often be of benefit to the headteacher and to the school in providing an opportunity to see and hear how other schools function.

One problem is that of being out of school too frequently and for too long, particularly where a headteacher becomes involved with a number of activities taking place in school time. Some meetings will be necessary and unavoidable, but there will be others where there is a measure of choice about becoming involved. A headteacher needs to develop criteria for deciding whether to attend outside activities and to be firm about this. An important criterion is whether the school will benefit in any way from the headteacher's involvement in the activity in question. Another is whether the headteacher has something valuable to offer to the particular activity. There is also the question of how well the senior staff are able to manage the school, although it is in some senses a criticism of the headteacher if he or she feels that a deputy is incapable of managing the school in his or her absence.

There is also a difference between the beginning of head-teachership when a headteacher cannot afford to be much out of school and later stages where there is a competent deputy and everything is running more or less smoothly.

Support governors in developing their work

The Education Reform Act has changed radically the relative roles of LEA, headteachers and governors. In particular headteachers now work with their governing bodies in ways which are different from those of the past. Governors, for their part, need to establish confidence in the headteacher's ability in the first instance and the headteacher will need to bear in mind the possible differences in outlook until headteacher and governors are well known to each other. A new headteacher needs to go about change carefully, sounding out governors as well as staff.

A legal framework for governors in their responsibilities for staff was provided under *S222 of the Education (Modification of Enactments Relating to Employment) Order 1988* which came into force in 1989 and which included the following provisions:

- Governors were given a share in the duties and responsibilities of employers.
- The governing body will have to appear as the respondent at industrial tribunals for any cases brought as a result of its action or by the LEA at its instruction, although governors will not be personally responsible for costs arising from any decision. The order does not affect staff in voluntary aided schools.
- A local dispute between staff working at the school and the governing body is now to be regarded as a trade dispute, provided the action falls within the definition of a trade dispute contained in the legislation.
- Trade unions will be able to organise industrial action against the governing body with immunity from civil action by the governors, provided that the action itself is lawful.
- The LEA will continue to have primary responsibility under the Health and Safety at Work Act (1974) and will be able to issue directions on health and safety with which schools must comply. Governors are responsible for the safety of employees.

(DES 1988a)

The responsibilities of the governing body

The responsibilities of the governing body now include the following:

- agreeing the aims and objectives of the school with the headteacher and staff
- agreeing the budget
- agreeing policies for the National Curriculum and its relation to LEA policy, and making sure they are implemented

- agreeing policies, and ensuring that they are implemented, for other aspects of curriculum, including
  - health and safety
  - sex education
  - religious education
  - public relations
  - admissions
  - equal opportunities
  - discipline
  - charging
- receiving and acting upon inspection reports
- agreeing arrangements for staff development
- agreeing arrangements for school evaluation
- appointing staff
- dealing with staff disciplinary cases
- ensuring that all governors are trained for their responsibilities
- evaluating their own work

Roles and relationships

Joan Sallis, in a paper delivered at a DES conference on governors, spoke of the relationship between headteachers and governors. She said that she believed that sound relationships could only be built on shared values, common purposes, efficient working structures and clarity about roles. The most difficult problems arise over territory which was until recently the professionals' preserve. Headteachers need to see their governors' work as a reflection of their management skills, and be professionally proud of it. This means having high expectations of their governors and sharing responsibility for their development. It is a considerable test of the headteacher's management skills to ensure a proper involvement of the governing body in the decision making process of the school and in the development of a school philosophy.

Headteachers can foster the work of governors in the following ways:

- encouraging them to set objectives and work towards them
- encouraging them to develop routines and systems for reviewing the work of the school
- taking issues to them at the sketch plan stage so that they play a part in the decision making process. For example, they should

be involved in the progress and updating of the school development plan

- helping to plan their involvement with the school so that their
  visits are purposeful and visiting governors have a clear
  programme
- making sure that governors have the opportunity to meet and
  get to know the work of the staff, perhaps by giving senior
  members of staff the chance to attend a governors' meeting to
  talk about their work
- ensuring that governors are aware of a range of techniques for
  appointing staff and that they employ good practice in undertaking this
- making opportunities to talk with every governor and not only
  those with whom the headteacher feels an affinity
- explaining his/her personal philosophy to them and demonstrating how it works out in practice as a preliminary to developing a joint philosophy
- encouraging them to take part in governor training and using
  all the possible opportunities to complement this by involving
  them in work in school and in appropriate staff meetings
- encouraging them to evaluate their work against objectives in a
  systematic and regular way
- establishing and communicating high expectations from
  governors

The relationship between headteacher and chair of governors is
particularly important. There must be a sharing of values and
mutual trust. Where these do not exist, it is important to do
everything possible to work towards them. There should be recognition by both parties of the other's role.

It is essential that the headteacher and chair keep each other
informed, probably by having a regular meeting. The headteacher
has to learn to be selective here, however, and to find out from
discussion what it is important for the chair to know. They need to
give similar messages about the school's aims and philosophy to
parents and the community.

Getting to know the school

Governors need to get to know the school well, from the inside as
well as from the outside. This means that they must visit while the

school is in action and become involved in some of its activities. This may be difficult for some governors and everything possible should be done to make suitable opportunities.

It can be difficult to be a visitor to a school if one does not know what is expected. It is very important that the headteacher and staff plan governors' visits carefully and make clear their expectations. A governor might:

- spend time in particular classes observing what is happening. It will be helpful here to suggest what the governor might look out for and to explain in advance what the teacher is trying to do;
- adopt classes or year groups or departments so long as this does not preclude their getting to know other aspects of the school's work;
- join the staff for field study work, helping to supervise the students;
- join the staff for a staff development day on an appropriate topic;
- join a staff working party with a particular task, for example, working out a programme for social and personal education or pastoral care;
- join the staff in evaluating a particular aspect of the life of the school;
- talk to the staff about a particular skill or knowledge he or she possesses, which might be of value to the school, or, if more appropriate, work with a group of students.

All LEAs have provided opportunities for governors' training and there are also many training packages. The headteacher can do much not only to encourage governors to become involved with training, but also to train governors in unobtrusive ways. All of the suggestions for involvement given above have a strong element of training.

Training for governors will need to be an on-going process as new governors become involved in the work. While much of the responsibility for this will remain with the LEA, it is important that both the governing body itself and the school play a part, particularly in the induction of new governors into the local situation.

The West Sussex newsletter for governors (West Sussex Education Committee 1991) suggests that each governing body appoints a 'link governor' with a responsibility for training. Among the other responsibilities suggested for this role is that of working with the headteacher to develop a pack of materials for new governors.

Governors need skills and knowledge in the following areas and headteachers should look for opportunities which help develop them; the more knowledgeable the governing body the more effectively it can support the school:

- selection and appointment of staff
- personnel issues, including staff discipline
- financial aspects of LMS
- other aspects of school management from the governors' point of view
- the National Curriculum
- other aspects of the curriculum, particularly:
  - sex education
  - religious education
  - economic and industrial understanding
  - careers education and guidance
  - health and safety
  - personal and social education
  - citizenship
  - environmental education
- special educational needs
- equal opportunities
- student welfare
- public relations
- chairmanship and effective meetings
- assessment and evaluation in schools

Evaluation

Governing bodies, like schools, need to evaluate their work from time to time, particularly in relation to the annual parents' meeting. Those in a position to evaluate are the governors themselves, the headteacher and teaching staff of the school and to some extent the parents, who will really be evaluating the work of the school. The headteacher can do much to encourage this kind of review. Evaluation may involve the following:

1 Looking at how objectives have been achieved.
2 Discussing areas of work and expressing satisfaction or dissatisfaction, e.g. reviewing the appointments made and discussing with the headteacher how successful they have been.

3 Circulating questionnaires to relevant groups, e.g. the governors themselves, headteacher, teachers and a sample of parents asking for comment about specific aspects of the governing body's work.
4 Questioning headteachers, teachers and a sample of parents about aspects of the governing body's work. It is sometimes useful to follow up questionnaires with discussion with relevant parties about the issues raised by the questionnaire survey.
5 Setting new objectives in the light of the evaluation

Readers interested in following this further should see the paper *Building an Effective School Governing Body*, published by the National Association of Governors and Managers, Paper 24, 1988. This gives a full list of the questions which governors might ask themselves about their work.

Involve parents where appropriate

One of today's problems about communication with parents which was rare in the past is that there may now be a number of children with three or four 'parents'. Under the Children's Act 1992, a parent of a dissolved partnership may seek from the courts joint parental rights. When these are granted he or she must be given access to school reports, invited to school functions and in all respects treated as equal with the partner who is parenting. Where a partner has not been granted these rights, the school may be in breach of the law in communicating with that partner unless the other partner specifically requests it. Divorced parents usually have equal rights. The new partner only has rights if the child is legally adopted. In such a case the new parent may well supercede the birthright parent. The school needs to be clear about the situation in the case of any child where there has been separation.

One important effect of the National Curriculum is that parents are being given a much clearer picture of how their children are doing in school. This has implications for all teachers who may now need to work more closely with parents than ever before.

Many schools have developed excellent work with parents but research suggests that there is still quite a way to go if schools are to create the kind of cooperation with parents which will truly support their children's learning. Atkin *et al.* suggest that when parents understand what the school is trying to do, identify with its goals and support it efforts, understand something of their roles as educators and take an interest in and provide support for their children's school work, then the effects can be both dramatic and long-lasting. They state that 'parents are an essential resource and also have unique opportunities as educators' (Atkin *et al.* 1988). The school needs to harness this resource for students' learning.

Both parents and teachers have stereotypes of each other and the parents' view of teachers will be largely formed by their own experience of school. This has left some people very hesitant about entering a school and talking with their children's teachers. Parents may see teachers as the fount of all knowledge and wisdom, as intimidating figures, as friends or as rather underpaid employees. Teachers, for their part, often blame parents for the problems their children create in school and frequently comment that it is the parents who do not come to school whom they would most like to see. Teachers may also hold the view that working-class parents are not particularly interested in their children's progress at school and this is particularly so where black parents are concerned. However, Tizard *et al.* noted that while 70 per cent of teachers in their study made negative comments about black parents, these were mainly to the effect that they were 'over-concerned with their children's education', 'had too high expectations', 'lacked understanding of British education' and so on (Tizard *et al.* 1988). The same study found that virtually all parents said they gave their children help with school work and more black than white parents started to teach their children to read before they started school. Although this is a study of primary rather than secondary school students, it would suggest that there are really very few parents who are not interested in their children's progress but some are hesitant about coming to the school to meet teachers. Asian mothers in particular may have limited English and be chary of male teachers and in consequence do not feel able to come to the school. It may be necessary to make special arrangements for them.

Atkin *et al.* (Atkin *et al.* 1988) suggest that schools do not give parents enough of the right sort of information. Parents get their ideas of what the school is doing mainly from their children and from looking at their work. They may not be aware of the educa- tional philosophy of the school, its policies and teaching strategies. Teachers too rarely explain what the term's work will consist of and suggest ways in which parents might help. Nor do they explain the processes by which they are helping students to learn. In general parents tend to get the message that teachers would rather they left the business of educating children to them. In practice many parents try to help and this help is a resource which is too rarely harnessed.

Tizard and her colleagues found that teachers did not give a great deal of feedback on children's progress. They were concerned to find that only 20 per cent of parents had been told that their child was having difficulties when testing suggested that the overall figure was considerably higher. Only 12 per cent of reception parents had been told that their child posed behaviour problems although the teachers said that 26 per cent of children posed such problems. There was also the feeling on the part of some parents that teachers tended to be defensive about problems rather than being prepared to discuss them openly. This pattern should gradually change as a result of the requirement to feed back information about progress in the National Curriculum.

Carrington and Short suggest a number of ways in which the school may contribute, perhaps unwittingly, to the non-involvement of parents. This may happen when:

- teachers are unwilling to work with parents who are regarded as non-professional and therefore not qualified to offer anything;
- teachers foster the view that the parents' responsibilities cease at the school gate;
- the school structures visiting arrangements for parents in such a way that some parents are prevented from coming by work commitments.

(Carrington and Short 1989)

Parents as partners

If parents are really treated as partners in the education of their children then they should have some involvement in some aspects of decision making. At the very least they should be consulted about appropriate aspects of change.

Atkin and her colleagues give a list of concerns and suggestions:

1 The development of practical arrangements for effective communication between parents, teachers and students lies at the heart of good home/school relationships. Parents need to see, discuss and experience and develop understanding.
2 Effective basic communication needs to be backed up by a range of appropriate opportunities for parents to participate in their children's schooling.

3 Schools need to recognise, support and strengthen the crucial role of parents as educators.
4 Parents represent a valuable but often unacknowledged resource which can be tapped to great effect in the education of children and young people.

(Atkin *et al.* 1988)

One might add that open days which give parents a chance to see what is happening are valuable as are opportunities for parents to experience some of the learning which their children are experiencing. Schools also need to give thought to ways in which parents can support students in different aspects of curriculum and ways of involving parents in appropriate decisions. 'Appropriate' here means more than decisions about issues such as school uniform. Some decisions about curriculum and organisation may be more effective if the school is aware of what parents think about them.

It would be very difficult to involve the parents of a secondary school in decision making in any substantial way, but it is possible to consult parents in groups, sometimes by inviting sample groups of parents to take part in some aspect of discussion, sometimes by involving all those who choose to come to talk in small, teacher-led groups about their ideas on particular issues, sometimes by sending questionnaires to samples of parents and making it clear that over a child's school life all parents will have the opportunity to take part in a questionnaire survey.

If parents are really going to be partners in their children's education they need to be taken into the confidence of the school more than is often the case. The DES papers *Planning for School Development 6* (1989) and *Development planning 7* (1991a) suggest that parents should be made aware of the school development plan and that governors should report on its progress at the annual parents' meeting. Many of the plans for learning need to be discussed with parents. At the level of the individual subject, each department needs to consider how to inform parents about the work being planned. There is much to be said for meetings of parents of one year at a time when the staff can talk about the work the students will be doing and the way in which parents can help with it. Methods need to be explained as well as outcomes so that parents can learn how to work with their children in ways which complement the work the teachers are doing. There is also a need for plenty of time for questions and discussion.

These studies all suggest that there is much to be gained from treating parents as partners in the education of their children and the school needs continually to be thinking of ways to do this. If the large majority of parents are keen to help their children to do well in school, this is a resource which teachers would do well to use. Parents who are keen to help their children will do this anyway, however much teachers discourage them. While it can be argued that some of the work of today's secondary school will be beyond the understanding of some parents, there is always something which parents can contribute if the school is prepared to look for it.

Communication with parents

Parents have a unique view of their children which is much more comprehensive than a teacher's can possibly be. Teachers have therefore much to learn from parents about the children they teach, but usually little opportunity is provided for this. What is needed is a regular meeting where both teachers and parents inform each other. The parents inform the teacher about the child and how they view what seems to be happening in school and the teacher informs the parents about the progress that child is making, the work which the child's class will be doing and how they can help. Both teacher and parents also need opportunities to discuss frankly the problems they are encountering and how they can work together to overcome them. It involves listening on the part of the teacher as well as on the part of the parent.

The studies suggest that there are two further ways in which teachers are not always effective in communicating with parents. In talking about how parents can help they tend to dwell on what not to do, rather than on what to do. They are also inclined to use what parents see as educational jargon. The problem about jargon is that one person's jargon is another person's technical language. Teachers quite properly have ways of talking about what they do which are particular to the education profession but are confusing to other people. It is a good idea for a group of teachers to try to think of all the words and phrases they use which will be seen by others as jargon. For example, topic work, environmental studies, records of personal achievement, TVEI, CDT, not to mention all the language which has come in with the Educational Reform Act – key stages, levels, Statements of Attainment, Attainment Targets, SATs and many other words, phrases and acronyms are unfamiliar to parents because they have all come into being since they were at school themselves. Such terms need either explaining or avoiding.

Teachers may also like to consider a year group newsletter which informs parents about the work in hand and how parents can help. This might also include information about school journeys and visits and what is needed for them as well as what may be needed for different aspects of other work. It will, of course, be important not to cover the same ground as any school newsletter and it may be necessary again to enlist the help of certain parents to translate the letter into other languages.

The major piece of communication with parents is now the discussion of each child's progress. Teachers must inform parents where their children have reached in the National Curriculum and although this can be done on paper, there should also be a meeting at which the details of what is being said can be explained.

Assessing the National Curriculum suggests that the intentions behind reporting are as follows:

- to widen access to information about the school's curriculum plans and objectives for individual students and classes in the case of parents and more generally for the school as a whole;
- to provide parents with the information necessary to support an informed dialogue with the school and with the children themselves about their achievements, progress and future work throughout their school career;
- to encourage partnership between schools and parents by sharing information and explaining its implications;
- to enable a school to report on the overall accomplishments of its students in ways that not only parents but also the wider community can appreciate.

(SEAC 1990)

Most teachers will regard it as important that students see their progress in the light of their own performance and tend to discourage too much comparison with other students. However, parents will certainly want to know, not only where their child stands currently, but how he or she stands in relation to other children of the same age. In most cases this will be a fairly complex picture with individual students being well up with the age group or beyond it for some work and doing less well in other areas.

The outcomes of National Curriculum testing will require quite a lot of explanation if parents are to understand about Levels and

Attainment Targets but it helps to answer questions about how the child stands in relation to other students because it can readily be seen that the answer is a complex one. Every student will have a different profile.

Discussion of this profile needs to be followed up by discussion of what teachers and parents can do to help the child in the areas where he or she is at the lower levels. The teacher who discusses this with parents needs to have some positive suggestions about ways in which the parents can help and to give them a clear idea of what he or she is planning to do.

It is important in these discussions to keep a positive view in all that is said. Teachers need to emphasize the areas in which the child is doing well and be positive about action to be taken where he or she is doing less well. They should also try to avoid over-stressing what not to do and concentrate instead on what parents can do.

Discussions with each child's parents need to go further than discussion about curriculum progress by including any problems of behaviour. Teachers, not unnaturally, feel that this is a very delicate area which could imply that either they or the parents are not doing their job. Tizard and her colleagues report that in the one in four cases where teachers actually discussed behaviour with parents 35 per cent of parents responded positively; 36 per cent agreed with the teacher; 25 per cent responded negatively and 15 per cent could not see the problem. There was also a marked difference between the views of parents and teachers. Only 30 per cent of children regarded as a problem by teachers were also thought a problem by parents and only 34 per cent of those seen as problems by parents were also seen as problems by teachers (Tizard *et al.* 1988). This suggests that children often differ in their behaviour between home and school and that there is everything to be gained from parents and teachers each knowing about the problems the others find and working together to overcome them. Parents are also often grateful for the opportunity to discuss with someone else the problems they encounter.

It has been customary for most discussions about students to take place on the school premises. However, there is much to be said for visiting the students' homes to discuss them with their parents. Parents feel more confident on their own ground and usually appreciate the fact that a teacher has taken the trouble to come to see them. This kind of meeting can be more relaxed than a meeting in school where there may be others waiting to see the teacher and it gives an opportunity for the teacher to learn about the parents' view of the child. A teacher can also learn a great deal about a child by seeing his or her home setting and the discussion tends to be more valuable than it sometimes is at school. This activity takes time but is very rewarding. It is important in doing this for the teacher to acquire techniques for finishing a meeting so that he or she does not spend too long in any one home. Usually putting one's papers together and making summarising statements give an indication that the meeting is ending.

Schools now have to send parents a written report on students' progress, a practice which has always been common in secondary schools. This needs to state where each child has reached in the National Curriculum and also report on other areas of work and such areas as work skills, behaviour, attitudes and any problems. It must also give information about the average class performance. Decisions about the nature of such reports will be made at school level, but parents may profitably be involved in discussing the design of the report form. Again it will be important to be positive as well as honest and there is much to be said for a report which allows parents to comment and, with older students, possibly allows them to comment also.

Parents in the classroom

It has become common practice in primary schools to invite parents to help in the classroom or about the school. This has a lot of advantages in that parents begin to see how teaching takes place and this not only helps them to support their own children, but may well make them good advocates for the school. The teacher is also helped in many of the tasks which take time from the more professional aspects of teaching. This is less common in secondary schools, but there are many ways in which parents can help the school, both in the classroom and more generally. For example, some schools have used parents to help students with learning difficulties, providing reading practice in a one-to-one situation, discussing what the student finds difficult and collaborating with the teacher to support the work in hand. Parents are also often used in the library. Where schools have parents who are highly competent in a foreign language through birth, residence or study, there may be a case for supervised conversation with older students in that language. The school which is determined to involve parents will find many opportunities to do so.

There are also problems. The first and most difficult problem is that of whether the school selects the parents who come in to help or takes all comers. Where parents are selected this can lead to bitterness and upset, but avoids the problem of the parent who wants to take over or the parent who is not very literate. On the other hand, it may be that the kinds of parents who are not selected are just those who would benefit most from being in the school and working with teachers. The problem of the parent who appears to want to take over may disappear if the teacher is clear what he or she wants and the problem of literacy is partly a matter of the tasks parents are asked to do. However, this too is something of a problem since there are inferences to be made from the tasks which are allocated to parents. It is also important to stress to parents helping in the school the need for confidentiality about the work of children other than their own.

In inviting parents to work in school, it will be important to discover what any individual parent can offer. A parent may have special knowledge and skills which could be used very widely in the school. It is also important to plan the work of parents and any other ancillary help in considerable detail. Bennett and Kell make the point that, in many of the classes they observed, ancillary helpers and parents were left to their own devices and in some cases were not supporting the teacher in a very satisfactory way because the teacher had not thought out how to use their services (Bennett and Kell 1989).

The non-statutory guidance in English (DES 1989) suggests that bilingual parents might help by reading and tape-recording stories in the home language of children in the class and then work with them to assist in translating the story into English.

A teacher who has parents helping in the classroom needs to think out in detail what they are to do and how they should react to students. This needs discussion among the staff so that all teachers are aware of their responsibilities in involving parents in the class-room. This all suggests that teachers need tactfully to give parents some training in some aspects of helping in the classroom. It may be best to ask them to undertake tasks like preparing materials in the first instance and gradually to involve them with students.

The needs of teachers in working with parents

Teachers are not trained to work with parents and, if this work is to be effective, time needs to be spent considering how best to deal with the various contacts. Work with parents could well be the topic for an in-service day, perhaps involving a number of parents during some part of the time. This might include:

- discussion about how to work with parents in the classroom and the drawing up of a policy about what should be done by way of ensuring that this help is well used;
- consideration of ways in which parents could be asked to do more to help their children with school work;
- study of the communications going to parents, looking to see whether they are free from jargon and clearly and well set out. Parents might be involved in this discussion;
- work on how to set about discussions with parents, particularly where students are not doing well. Role playing may be a good way of trying out approaches to different types of parents. Parents might be involved in this, giving feedback about how they experienced the way teachers tackled the interviews;
- the preparation of questions to ask parents invited for part of the day to talk with teachers about their views. The teachers might work in small groups, each group with a different set of questions about how parents see matters. The parents then spend a short time with each group answering their questions;
- work on drawing up an overall school policy about working with parents so that there is guidance for the future.

Establish relationships with employers

Secondary schools now need to have good relationships with employers in order to provide places for work experience. They also need to draw on any sponsorships that they can. More fundamentally, there is a need for staff and students to understand the world of business and industry, for the school to prepare students for future employment and for people in business and industry to understand what goes on in schools.

Time is the problem for both employers and for the staff of the school and contacts must be carefully planned so that those concerned gain the maximum from them. Many schools have governors with industrial experience who may be able to help in developing links. Most schools also have a member of staff with responsibility for organising work experience and there is much to be said for having a small working group of staff, someone from local industry and possibly governors or parents to foster the relationships between the school and local business and industry. Activities might include some of the following:

- secondment of staff to a local firm to undertake a specific task. For example, one school seconded a modern language teacher to help the firm to develop materials for their overseas market;
- secondment of staff for a short period to shadow a manager in a local firm;
- secondment of someone from industry to spend time in school looking at specific aspects of work and talking to young people;
- provision by local industry of a problem for students to work at. This would involve their visiting the firm and getting to know as much as possible about the context of the task they are to undertake. It might also involve the secondment of someone from the firm or regular visiting by that person in order to see that the work being undertaken was appropriate and likely to be of value;
- involvement with school staff or local advisory staff of someone from a local firm in evaluation of an appropriate aspect of work in the school;
- involvement of someone from industry to give students practice in being interviewed;
- industrial visits linked with some aspect of the curriculum;
- contacts by individual departments with appropriate local industries and use of projects and materials stemming from their work for work with students;
- mini-enterprise schemes;
- involvement of someone from local industry in a staff in-service day on an appropriate topic which helps staff to understand the needs of industry;
- survey of local industry by students;
- involvement of local industry in the development of records of achievement;
- making links with any local organisations concerned with school/industry links, for example, SATRO (Science and Technology Regional Organisation).

Fullick stresses the importance of establishing trust on both sides in developing industrial links if the links are to be valuable and lasting. He therefore suggests that the agenda set should be mutual with representatives from industry and teachers working together (Fullick 1992).

Encourage the use of the community for learning

Learning needs to be transferable. What students learn in school is useful only if they can apply it in situations outside the school. The world outside the school is thus both the source of material for learning and also the end to which learning must be directed.

The local community and environment provide much valuable learning material for students. They are a vital source of material for subjects such as history and geography which are partly about the development of communities and their interaction with their environment. Much material for scientific and mathematical learning is present in the local environment. It provides a basis for creative work in writing, drama, dance, art and music.

There is also a need to help students feel a responsibility for their local environment, for improving it, trying to keep it free of pollution and vandalism, helping to make it a good place to be. This means developing understanding of how local government works and the ways in which people can contribute locally.

Chapter 16

Evaluation

Evaluation in school is an extension of the everyday task of weighing up situations and people and making assessments in order to make decisions about action. In making professional judgements we need to be more _objective_ and to think clearly about the judgements we make. We evaluate in order to assess past action and learn from it, ready for new planning and action. _Evaluation implies a setting against values._ This suggests that assessment might be regarded as a stage in evaluation where information is collected in order to compare it with standards of some kind.

Evaluation is required for four main purposes in schools:

1 _The support of individual development_: students need to know how they are doing in order to improve. The teacher's assessment of individual pieces of work, and of work and behaviour generally, helps the students to see progress and establish internal standards so that they eventually become self-reliant adults. The general comments may be part of a profile system to which students also contribute or simply teachers' comments on the work of students. There will also be statements about how students have done in SATs.

   Teachers also need to know how they are doing, especially at the early stages of their careers, and this is the purpose of the appraisal system.

2 _The management of students' learning_: students have to be organised into groups for learning, very often on the basis of grouping those who are at similar stages of learning. Evaluation is therefore needed both at the school level and within individual classes.

Matching groups of students to teachers also requires some evaluation of the ability of the teacher.

3 *Accreditation for students and teachers*: accreditation is provided for students in various forms. The most obvious one is that of examination performance, but schools also provide written references and records of achievement built up over a period.

Schools also provide accreditation for teachers in the form of reports upon those seeking promotion.

4 *Accountability*: schools are accountable to the community through their governors for providing for the needs of their students with the resources they are able to make available from the budget they are given. There is an increasing need to make public what a school is achieving and the introduction of four-yearly inspections and the publication of reports on these as well as the publication of examination results and other information make the school's achievement very public. The task for the individual school will then be to interpret this information to parents and the community.

OFSTED

Evaluation can be undertaken internally by teachers or externally by inspectors and advisers, possibly with assistance from governors, parents and others who may look with a rather different perspective. It may involve evaluation of individuals or groups or the whole school.

Although the processes of evaluation for different purposes may sometimes be similar and, in some situations, evaluation made for one purpose may service another, this is not always the case. For example, assessments made to help the learning of less able students need to be positive and to stress what they can do as well as identifying the areas in which they still need to learn. It is unhelpful to such students to compare them with their more able peers. But a comparison with the peer group may be needed in order to place students in groups for learning and it will be important in this context not to discourage the less able to the extent that they give up trying. It is therefore helpful in reviewing the school's evaluation procedures to keep these four aspects of evaluation in mind.

Evaluation depends upon indicators of performance. A teacher can make judgements about what a student knows and can do only from what the student says and does. The success of a change in organisation or of curriculum development must be evaluated on the basis of such indicators as the views expressed about it, the improvement in the students' behaviour or learning. Issues such as improvement in behaviour need to be defined closely so that there is agreement on what evidence demonstrates them. Some indicators such as test results or the collection of views require particular activity as part of the evaluative process, such as consideration of specific questions or the use of interviews, questionnaires or check lists. Other indicators such as absence rates, statistics about choice of subject, examination statistics or staying on rates may be collected for a different purpose but may be used as evaluative material.

The introduction of regular inspections does not take the place of the school's own evaluation of its activities. The process of inspection will be more valuable if the school has conducted its own review, is aware of the areas which need attention and can provide the inspection team with information about issues which are in the school development plan because they have arisen from the school's own evaluation of its work.

Evaluation must involve consideration of what the school and the individual teachers are trying to do. Aims and objectives require formulation and it is at the planning stage of any activity that thought should be given to evaluation.

The evaluation tasks of management are to:

1 Establish a policy for assessment and evaluation.
2 Ensure regular evaluation of the school.

Establish a policy for assessment and evaluation

The school policy for assessment and evaluation should include statements of the following:

- the aspects of school life which will be evaluated systematically and the way in which this will be done
- the evaluation programme
- the use to be made of student records
- the system for assessing and marking students' work
- examinations policy
- the programme for developing evaluative skills in students
- staff responsibilities for evaluation

Ensure regular evaluation of the school

It is the task of management to see that evaluation policy is carried out. This means designing a system which ensures that over a period all the different aspects of the life and work of the school are evaluated.

Assessment and evaluation primarily concern the work of all teachers, since effective teaching depends upon the teacher's ability to assess the learner's needs, capacity and response. The testing of the National Curriculum makes this easier to do but there is still a need for continuous assessment of the work of students. The headteacher and senior staff need to see that teachers also evaluate their own work and keep clear records of work undertaken and learning achieved, both in order to antici- pate need and to assess progress. There is a case for staff agreeing that they will all keep a particular kind of record of their own work so that teachers joining the staff permanently or on supply can draw on the records of their predecessors. There is also a need for evaluation of the broader aspects of school life, such as pastoral care, behaviour, parental relationships and similar aspects.

Evaluation in school might be expected to cover the items in the list shown in Figure 16.1, looking at them in the light of the overall aims of the school and the school development plan. Space is left beside each item to suggest possible indicators. Individual schools will also wish to add more items.

Designing the evaluation system

This involves:

Making a plan which covers the ground over a period It is self-evident that it is not possible for any school to evaluate all its work in a short period of time. A school needs to have a cycle of evaluation planned over a period of several years in which items listed are evaluated regularly, with some being dealt with more frequently according to current need. The school's own evaluation will be complemented by the four-yearly inspection programme. Evalua- tion needs to be built into any new developments and there should be an annual programme of evaluation which asks for assessment of various aspects of the life and work of the school at different times during the year.

In making this plan it is wise to allow time for action following each aspect of work evaluated. There is little point in evaluation if it is not followed by action on the findings.

	Assessments required	Performance indicators
Curriculum	The relationship of the curriculum philosophy to the curriculum as taught	
	The development and progress of students	
	The effectiveness of the learning and teaching	
	Provision for students with special needs including the very able	

	Continuity
	    within the school
	    with contributory schools
	    with schools/colleges to which
	    students transfer	

	Preparation for adult life	
Organisation	The effectiveness of the timetable	
	Overall organisation of the school into groups for learning	
	The effectiveness of the management structure	

	Staff organisation
	The use of time by
	    students
	    teachers
	    non-teaching staff	

	The life of the school including:
	    assemblies
	    lunch times
	    out of school activities
	    special events, e.g. plays, concerts	

Figure 16.1 Assessments and performance indicators

	Assessments required	Performance indicators

Planning	The effectiveness of:
	  planning
	  decision making patterns
	  budget management	

	The extent and success of innovaton	
Pastoral care	Pastoral organisation	
	Effectiveness of educational guidance	
	Pupil behaviour and discipline	
	Record keeping	
	Reports to parents	
Teaching staff	The recruitment of teachers	
	Staff deployment	
	Staff performance	
	Professional development of teachers	
	Staff records	

Non-teaching staff	Work of non-teaching staff including:
	  office and clerical staff
	  library staff
	  technicians
	  caretaking and cleaning staff
	  kitchen and dining room staff	

Figure 16.1 (Continued)

	Assessments required	Performance indicators

Communication	The effectiveness of communicatin with:
	   students
	   teachers
	   non-teaching staff
	   parents
	   governors
	   contributory schools
	   transfer schools and colleges
	   employers	

Relationships	Relationships
	   student/student
	   students/teachers
	   teacher/teacher
	   parents/teachers
	   teachers/governors
	   school/contributory schools
	   school/transfer schools and
	      colleges
	   school/employers	

Evaluation	Use of marking system	
	Testing	
	Teacher records	
	Arrangements for school review	

Management	The personal organisation and effectiveness of:
	   senior management
	   middle management	

Accom/resources	Accommodation/grounds
	   physical state
	   cleanliness
	   attractiveness	

	State of resources	

Figure 16.1 (Continued)

Involving staff, students, parents and governors Teachers in secondary schools are normally involved in the process of evaluating the work of students. They also need to be involved in self-evaluation, as teachers, as form tutors and in management roles – a process which appraisal should assist. Students should also be involved in the evaluation process, helping to identify the questions which might be asked, discussing their experience as learners, completing questionnaires on their views and perhaps undertaking some evaluation as part of their normal work, using databases and spreadsheets to analyse some of their findings.

Samples of parents need to be involved in various aspects of the school's evaluation programme. Sometimes this will be a matter of inviting a small group of parents to discuss some aspect of school. Sometimes a questionnaire might be sent to a particular year group or area. Parent governors should also provide useful information.

Governors have an important part to play in the evaluation programme. They should be involved in drawing up the programme and in receiving reports on what has been discovered. They may also be able to provide independent views on some aspects of school life.

The processes of evaluation

These require consideration of the following points:

1 There must be careful sampling. The evidence available for making an assessment is only a sample of what is being assessed, whether it is a consideration of what a student knows and can do, the skills of a particular teacher or the effectiveness of pastoral care in a school, or anything else. The sample must be representative of what is being assessed.
2 Assessments must be valid and reliable. Validity in making observations is increased if more than one person assesses the same material and observers come to similar conclusions. Reliability in observation is increased if observations are made of comparable situations on more than one occasion.
3 Assessments need to be both formative or summative.
4 An evaluator must look from different viewpoints. The point of the controversial inclusion of a lay person in Offsted inspection teams is to provide a different viewpoint. Schools and teachers may feel that work is going well but parents and possibly

governors may see their work very differently. There is also the problem that in observing what is happening in a school it is all too easy to see only from one's own point of view and to make inaccurate judgements about work which stems from a different viewpoint. Anyone observing teaching, for example, needs to know what the teacher intends to do if he or she is to make a judgement about the effectiveness of teaching.

5 Subjectivity and objectivity should be balanced. The subjective view of experienced practising teachers is known to be a good predictor of student performance. Subjective assessment has the advantage that it is faster and more comprehensive than some assessments which are apparently more objective. Human judgement nevertheless needs occasional checking against more objective forms of assessment. Assessment is made more objective by combining the subjective judgements of more than one person.

Approaches to evaluation

A school needs to consider various ways of evaluating and to choose those appropriate for the particular task. The following can be used:

Procedures based on observation and inspection   Teachers observe what their students do and say and question them in order to assess their progress and learning. The accuracy of judgements made in this way depends upon the skill with which the observation and questioning are carried out and the breadth of professional experience which the assessor brings to the interpretation of what is seen and heard.

This kind of assessment is made more objective by planning observations against a check list or by checking one person's observations against those of another. This is not always necessary but is sometimes useful.

Assessment by personal observation and questioning has also the advantage that a skilled and experienced observer can take into account many factors which are acknowledged to be important but which may not be easy to measure. For example, the contribution the school is making to the moral or aesthetic education of its students is probably most effectively assessed by observation.

This kind of assessment can also take into account many factors at once, so that in watching a class at work, an observer may note that the teacher is not only covering the syllabus effectively but also teaching the students how to study and solve problems.

In using this kind of assessment it is important to ensure that the views of students are investigated and used. This may be a matter of discussing with groups of students their reaction to the teaching they have received.

Questionnaires   Questionnaires to a sample of teachers, parents or students may yield useful information about various aspects of the life and work of the school. There should be some questions which are definite and can be analysed by computer as well as questions which allow for personal comment. It is always a good idea to pilot questionnaires with a small group in order to discover whether they produce information which is useful and also to investigate the best way to analyse them.

Test and examination results   All teachers devise tests for their own use and many use some form of standardised test material. SATs will also offer information.

Tests should ideally be selected according to purpose. National testing is mainly a matter of accountability but offers useful information to the teacher about students' learning. Other testing may be to discover the stage students have reached and whether they are ready for the next stage of learning or teaching. The tester might note not only what students know and can do but also how they set about a task. The teacher may test to discover which students have acquired the skill, knowledge or understanding required, how individual students perform relative to their peers, the difficulties individuals are experiencing and their nature, how students are best grouped for learning and the effectiveness of the teaching of a group.

At the end of secondary education, the public examination system yields valuable information both about students and about the teaching they have received. Results need to be explained to governors and parents, particularly in view of the publication of league tables. It is important that the school's examination policy is widely known and that there is information about the value added by the school. The information from SATs will make this easier to produce.

Records and statistics A school also needs records of personal achievement for students. These normally cover many aspects of school life and often involve assessments by students. They provide information for parents and for would-be employers as well as helping those concerned with career guidance.

There are also statistics about the school which should be on computer and which yield interesting information when analysed. Attendance records of both staff and students are obvious examples.

It is easy to see evaluation as concerned with ends rather than means, yet all our study of education in recent years suggests that the process by which learning takes place is as important as the content – a conclusion not always appreciated by laymen. This is much more difficult to assess than the learning of content. It involves looking at attitudes and learning skills. The overall success of teaching might be demonstrated by the number of students able to work independently by the time they leave school. How well will the average school leavers do if given a period of time to produce a piece of independent research with no help at all from a teacher? How will they do if given a problem which is not recognisably based in any given subject area but perhaps uses learning from several of them? How good are students at applying what they have learned in the world outside school? To what extent do students leaving school want to go on learning? What is their attitude to the various subjects they have studied in school? These are important criteria for judging how well a school is doing. Course work has helped students to become better at independent learning and work in technology has made them better problem solvers. Has there been any change in attitudes?

Finally we need to consider the role of the headteacher in evaluation. The headteacher must ensure that the evaluation policy and programme are in place and carried out. The headteacher is also an evaluator who is involved in identifying the problems and needs of the school community in order to do something about them. In theory the headteacher has greater opportunities for access to what is happening in all parts of the school than anyone else. In practice it is important to work at this. It can be done informally but it needs to be systematic.

The headteacher also needs to sample what is happening in classrooms, seeing all staff at work from time to time, working to make this a positive activity. He or she also needs to sample students' work, perhaps collecting in the notebooks of a particular group or sample of individuals. Following a student or group around for a morning or a day is also very valuable if a headteacher can find time to do it.

This kind of evaluation is all too easy to forget, given the many pressures that headteachers find themselves under today. But if the headteacher does not do these things, no one else will and important aspects of the school's life may be the poorer.

Chapter 17

Personal organisation

A headteacher or senior manager must not only perform management tasks competently and be skilled in different aspects of the role but also be able to organise so that personal time and energies are used to the best advantage. In today's schools this is far from easy. There have been considerable new demands on headteachers in recent years and no easing of previous demands to compensate. This makes the ability to manage time even more important. Being well organised is a matter of knowing oneself and having the self-discipline to maintain routines and priorities. One needs to know how to get the best out of oneself.

The use of time

To be well organised people need to know the times of day when they are at their best. Some people work best early in the morning; others late at night. Some people work best in short spells; others work better when they can have a long spell of uninterrupted time. This knowledge has implications for the best time for tackling difficult problems and work which is taxing.

None of us can increase the time we have. We can only look for better ways of using it. The meaning of the word 'better' in this context will depend upon what a person is trying to do. Once aims and priorities have been established a headteacher has a yardstick for assessing the way he or she is actually using time. A manager's achievement must in the end be measured by what actually happens as a result of his or her actions.

There are some tasks vested in the role of the leader, whether headteacher or at a lower level of seniority. For example, the headteacher represents the school to the outside world and time must be given to this. The headteacher is also the main point of contact for governors and the LEA. There are many occasions when the headteacher's agreement must be sought; occasions when he or she must function as the official leader of the school. A headteacher who opts out of any of these tasks may lose the confidence of the school community.

The headteacher also has a unique role as the ultimate authority in the school. This makes his or her praise and blame special and this is a part of the office which must be accepted and used for the good of the community.

The headteacher also has an important role in ensuring that there is adequate planning, development and evaluation and in seeing that the management tasks listed in the previous chapters are undertaken by someone. He or she must be aware of what is happening in the school and be seen frequently by teachers and students. This means being out of the office and around the school for some part of the school day. A headteacher also needs some time to get organised each day and time for personal refreshment. Sometimes the best way to deal with a problem is to lay it aside and seek relaxation.

It may sometimes seem as if the headteacher is at everyone's beck and call but there is still a substantial area of choice in the use of time and he or she has to make this time serve the priorities.

The starting point for improving the use of time is diary analysis. Every headteacher should take time to analyse his or her diary at regular intervals. It is also profitable to keep for a week or so a much fuller account of what happens, noting the time which is spent on planned and unplanned activities, tasks undertaken which could only be undertaken by the headteacher and those that could have been delegated. Diary analysis will make clear how much time there is available for planned activity.

Another analysis which yields useful information is a study of all the interruptions which occur during the course of a day. If a list of these is kept on several occasions it may become possible to see whether the number of interruptions could be decreased or whether some of them could be confined to a particular time of day. People differ in the extent to which they can accept interruptions, so this is a matter of personal style. It is important to be able to get uninterrupted time when it is necessary.

Many people find that, when they analyse their use of time, there is much that they feel they should be doing but have not the time to do and very little which they feel they can give up! This is where the priorities come in. It may be helpful to examine the following questions:

- How does the pattern of what is actually being done differ from the pattern of what should done?
- Is the headteacher's time being properly divided among people?
- How much time is planned and how much unplanned?
- What is getting interrupted?

The answers to these questions create further questions about how to find more time in an already over-full programme. What must be given up? How can more time be found? The following might be examined:

Level of accessibility

Accessibility to staff, parents and students is obviously an important aspect of the headteacher's role. When teachers and others speak of the headteacher as being accessible they usually mean first of all that if they want to ask a question related to their day-to-day work the headteacher is easy to find. In a small school this will not be too difficult. In a large school most of the day-to-day decisions should be taken by other senior staff and there should be only a limited need for the headteacher to deal with such matters.

In the second place accessibility is usually taken to mean that the headteacher is available and prepared to listen when an individual has a problem or a matter on which comment or advice is wanted. This is not always possible but accessibility is partly the attitude the headteacher demonstrates to other people. If he or she is normally receptive to them and their problems they will usually accept that there are times when the headteacher does not want to be interrupted. A teacher is likely to be happy to make an appointment to talk to the headteacher at length if it will normally be in circumstances where there is privacy and where the headteacher will concentrate on listening supportively. What such a teacher does not want is that the door is opened or the telephone rings frequently during the interview. The ability to ensure uninterrupted time when it is needed cannot be pursued at the same time as total accessibility. A balance is needed.

If a headteacher is too accessible there will be a tendency for people to come to him or her with matters which should properly go to other members of the management team. A headteacher has to be tough over this, particularly when new in office.

There is much to be said for a headteacher setting aside time which will only be interrupted for genuine emergencies. This will provide opportunity for concentrating on the needs of individuals and on matters such as forward planning. If a headteacher does this regularly and everyone knows that Wednesday afternoons, for example, are sacrosanct, this will be accepted.

Extent of delegation

Diary analysis will show the extent to which a headteacher is using time on jobs which are neither specifically part of the headteacher's role nor need the headteacher's personal abilities. If there are many of these, perhaps too little is delegated. A headteacher might note how often people come for advice or decisions. If this is happening too frequently there may be too little delegation or a lack of understanding by others of where the headteacher stands on a number of issues.

The efficiency of systems

A school needs systems which take everyone concerned the minimum time to implement for dealing with all recurring procedures. Senior management needs to see that information is fed out in a form which is easy to absorb for whatever purpose it is needed. Generally speaking computers are now providing for this.

The filing system needs to be organised so that others can find their way around it if the secretaries are absent and this will be particularly important for the headteacher's personal filing which should include a system for bringing forward material when it is needed. One solution is to have a file for each month of the year into which reminder notes are placed about matters which need to be checked in the future.

Standard and duplicated forms of communication help to use time well since they reduce to the minimum the writing necessary and ensure that all the information needed is given.

Material should normally be prepared for typing using a dictation machine, except where the material is very complex. It enables the person dictating to use odd moments effectively and it can be used anywhere.

The use of short periods of time

It is very easy to waste short periods of time and they add up to a considerable period over the course of a week. It is valuable to have a number of jobs which can be undertaken in the ten minutes before a visitor arrives or the quarter of an hour before lunch.

The time spent teaching

The headteacher of a secondary school is paid to lead the school community rather than to teach. This is not to say that the headteacher should not teach but that the time spent in teaching should be very limited, especially in a large school. The leadership role should come first and there should be a reason for undertaking teaching. A new headteacher may wish to demonstrate competence in the classroom and to get the feel of the school by teaching, sampling different groups of students. There may be occasions when the headteacher happens to be a specialist in a shortage area of curriculum. It must be remembered that it is extremely difficult for a headteacher to maintain a regular programme of teaching and students may suffer if he or she tries to take on too much.

Stress

Stress affects most people in education today. There are many reasons for this. A fundamental reason is that the government aims for education and the values these represent are at odds with the aims and values held by most teachers. Teachers generally do not see education as a form of competition and as a commodity to be purchased by the community but as a service and a liberating influence aimed at developing each child as an individual. The general tendency to denigrate the work of teachers and to attribute the success they achieve to other causes, such as examinations becoming easier, also contribute to stress. Headteachers are experiencing greater stress as a result of their greater responsibilities as well as their position at the boundary of the school where they must interact with the public and work with governors. Deputy headteachers are in a particularly stressful position in that they stand between the headteacher and the staff and are expected to mediate in situations where there is a difference.

What is stress? Kyriacou states: 'Teacher stress refers to the experience by teachers of unpleasant emotion such as anger, tension, frustration, depression and nervousness, resulting from their work as teachers' (Kyriacou 1989).

Martens gives a more complex definition: 'a process that involves the perception of a substantial imbalance between environmental demand and response capability, under conditions where failure to meet demand is perceived as having important consequences and is responded to with increased levels of anxiety' (Martens 1982).

Headteachers not only have to consider their own problems of stress but also those of their colleagues. Awareness that teachers are becoming stressed is important because this enables support to be given. It is also important to create a situation in which people feel free to discuss the problems they are experiencing without feeling that this is an admission of failure. People also feel less stressed when they are able to manage their time well and it may be worth spending a professional development day on time management.

Teacher stress can lead to teacher burnout, described by Kyriacou as follows:

Teacher burnout refers to a state of mental, emotional and attitudinal exhaustion which results from a long period of stress. Such teachers are still able to function as teachers, but they have largely lost their commitment and enthusiasm for their work and this inevitably shows in aspects of their job performance.

(Kyriacou 1989)

Mancini et al. found that burned out teachers gave 'significantly less information and less praise, showed less acceptance of their students' ideas and interacted less frequently with them' (Mancini et al. 1984). Burnout may lead to more serious forms of illness, such as depression and other psychological disorders and to prolonged absence from teaching or to people leaving the profession altogether.

Woods suggests that the following people are most at risk:

- probationers and inexperienced teachers who have not yet learned how to cope with the dilemmas and contradictions.of the teacher's role
- teachers lacking knowledge and understanding of student culture

- teachers who find it difficult to 'orchestrate their teaching' in the classroom
- senior teachers who are in a position of greater role conflict.

(Woods 1989)

Stress is affected by various aspects of the working environment. Where the demands on people are greater than they can reasonably expect to achieve, they are likely to experience stress. However, the extent to which individuals experience stress depends also on their personal resources. People who see themselves in charge of their lives are less likely to experience stress than those who see their lives directed by others. Stress is less likely to occur where people have been involved in decision making about the work they do and where there is strong support from colleagues and a problem-solving attitude in the school. The current experience of change beyond the control of the profession has resulted in considerable stress on many people.

Handy speaks of creating 'stability zones' which he describes as places for rebuilding energy reserves. Holidays and weekends, home and family, are important stability zones (Handy 1976). It is valuable for people to be able to turn to some quite different interest or occupation from time to time and there seems to be evidence that physical activity helps to combat stress, whether this is a strenuous game or a mild activity such as gardening. Making things also seems to offer a way of relaxing. Relaxation techniques and meditation have also been used as a way of managing stress.

It is not easy for those who are deeply involved in their professional lives to switch off and it may help to be able to talk through problems and difficulties with a friend or with one's partner. Handy also suggests that routines are a way of coping with stress, enabling a person to do some things without thinking about them because they are habits. Routines are particularly useful when a person is tired and flagging.

Headteachers and senior members of staff need to be preparing for the stressful situations when they are not under pressure. This is the time to organise the routines and the systems and arrange the delegation, the time to develop stability zones and hobbies and outside interests and activities. People who can organise their professional lives so that they run smoothly for most of the day, have time left for the problems and strategies to cope with the stressful situations.

Conclusion

This book sets out to explore some of the major issues involved in running a secondary school. The process is a complex one and there are probably as many good ways of carrying out this task as there are good headteachers. Each person has to select an appropriate path for himself or herself. The various analyses given are intended to help the reader to identify personal priorities and decide how best to work as a particular person in a given situation.

No action is isolated. Everything one does affects something and someone else. In seeking to achieve a particular development one may also help to achieve or hinder another. The headteacher of any school is at the centre of a complex pattern of relationships and communications so that what he or she does affects many others. A headteacher needs clear vision and the ability to transmit thinking and draw other people's ideas into a common vision so that the school community moves forward by a creative consensus. A headteacher also needs a wider view of the local community and a sense of being part of the total process of educating young people into the way of life of our society. This requires not only professional commitment but a sense of perspective.

Most people who achieve headship in secondary schools have clear ideas about education but they need to go on developing and modifying ideas and extending them in the light of experience as well as absorbing the changes coming from central government. A headteacher also needs to go on being a student and an enthusiast.

Leadership in a school involves liking not only young people but adults and enjoying working with them, confident in one's relationships and able to use the skills of leadership developed in the process of gaining experience in senior posts. A leader needs to be a good listener, able to interpret other people's behaviour and make each person feel that he or she really matters and has something of special value to contribute, and is skilled in helping teachers to develop their work and in guiding and counselling them.

To be a good headteacher one must be a good organiser. The headteacher must see that life in the school runs smoothly and that little time is wasted on minor matters. A headteacher needs skill in identifying and tackling problems, with strategies for helping others to meet and resolve difficulties, giving them confidence that there can be a satisfactory outcome to many problems and building on growth points. A good leader is good at delegating and ready to allow the staff to take decisions, helping them to think through to a conclusion and evaluate the consequences. One needs positive attitudes to change and development, even when it is unwelcome.

In all this it is important that a leader has good self-knowledge and is aware of personal limitations and fallibility as well as strengths, is self-critical and uses feedback from colleagues. A leader needs to be open-minded, recognising and using ideas appropriately whatever their source. One also needs to be well organised and able both to set and to maintain priorities. A leader who has a clear sense of direction, held rationally as well as intuitively, who has a balanced view and is able to stand back from the job, will be able to withstand pressure and cope with the stresses which are inevitable in headship. A headteacher needs both analytical skill and the ability to work intuitively, sensing how people feel and responding to them. It helps if one has creative ability in generating ideas to deal with new situations but one also needs to be ready to recognise and use the ideas of others.

This picture of the headteacher demands a mature and balanced human being who is knowledgeable, skilled and caring and able to undertake successfully all the tasks involved. Headship is difficult and demanding. We are fortunate as a nation in having so many people who are able to do well this difficult and demanding job.

References

Atkin, J., Bastiani, J. and Goode, J. (1988) *Listening to Parents*; London: Croom Helm.

Back, K. and Back, K. (1982) *Assertiveness at Work*; London: McGraw–Hill.

Beare, H., Caldwell, B.J. and Millikan, R.H. (1989) *Creating an Excellent School*; London: Routledge.

Bennett, N. and Kell, J. (1989) *A Good Start? Four-year-olds in infant schools*; London: Open Books.

Boulton, M.J. and Underwood, K. (1992) 'Bullying/victim problems among middle school children'; *The British Journal of Educational Psychology*, February.

Caldwell, B.J. and Spinks, J.M. (1988) *The Self-managing School*; Sussex: Falmer.

Carrington, B. and Short, G. (1989) *Race and the Primary School*; Windsor: NFER–Nelson.

Cave, E. and Wilkinson, C. (eds) (1990) *Local Management of Schools: some practical issues*; London: Routledge.

Cave, E. and Demick, D. (1990) 'Marketing the school' in Cave E. and Wilkinson C. (eds) *Local Management of Schools: some practical issues*; London: Routledge.

CIPFA/LGTB/SEO (1988) *The LMS Initiative: local management in schools: a practical guide*; London.

Cole, M. and Walker, S. (1989) *Teaching and Stress*; Milton Keynes: Open University Press.

Dean, J., Waddilove, J., Adams, D., Chanter, T. and Betteridge, D. (1984) *Where Am I Going?*; London: Schools Council.

Dean, J. (1991) *Professional Development in Schools*; Milton Keynes: Open University Press.

Department of Employment (1974) *Health and Safety at Work Act*; London: HMSO.

DES (1984) *Records of Achievement: a statement of policy*; London: HMSO.

DES (1986) *Education Act (No.2)*; London: HMSO.

DES (1987) *Circular 7/87*; London: Department of Education and Science.

DES (1988a) *S222 Education (Modification of Enactments Relating to Employ-ment)*; London: Department of Education and Science.

DES (1988b) *Education Reform Act*; London: HMSO.

DES (1989) *Planning for School Development (6): advice to governors, head-teachers and teachers*; London: Department of Education and Science.

DES (1989) *English in the National Curriculum: non-statutory guidance*; London: HMSO.

DES (1990) *Letter from Secretary of State to Chief Education Officers*, 10 December; London: Department of Education and Science.

DES (1991a) *Development Planning (7): a practical guide*; London: Department of Education and Science.

DES (1991b) *School Teacher Appraisal: circular 12/91*; London: Department of Education and Science.

Doe, B. (1992) 'How to make your school safe'; *TES*, 22 May.

Drucker, P. (1968) *The Practice of Management*; London: Pan Piper.

Elliott, J., Bridges, D., Gibson, R. and Nias, J. (1981) *School Accountability*; London: Grant McIntyre.

Fayol, H. (1949) *General and Industrial Management*; London: Pitman.

Fisher, R. and Ury, W. (1987) *Getting to Yes*; (4th ed.) London: Arrow Books.

Fletcher, M. (1991) 'In the market for understanding'; *TES Supplement*, 13 September.

Forster, P. (1991) 'Whose choice is it anyway?'; *Managing Schools Today* 1(6).

Foster, J. (1988) 'Equal opportunities' a lecture given at the annual conference of NAIEA, Bedford, 24 September.

Fullan, M. and Steigelbauer, S. (1991) *The New Meaning of Educational Change*; London: Cassell.

Fullick, P. (1992) 'Links with industry and employers' in Foskett N. (ed.) *Managing External Relations in Schools*; London: Routledge.

Galton, M. and Willcocks, J. (1983) *Moving from the Primary School Class-room: the Oracle study*; London: Routledge and Kegan Paul.

Hallinger, P. and Murphy, J. (1986) 'The social context of schools'; *American Journal of Education* 94(3).

Handy, C. (1976) *Understanding Organisations*; Harmondsworth: Penguin.

Hargreaves, D. (1982) *The Challenge of the Comprehensive School*; London: Routledge.

Hargreaves, D. (1984) *Improving Secondary Schools*; London: ILEA.

Harrop, A. and McCann, C. (1983) 'Behaviour modification and reading attainment in the comprehensive school'; *Educational Research* 25(3).

Herzberg, F., Mausner, B. and Snyderman, B. (1959) *The Motivation to Work*; New York: Wiley.

HMI (1978) *Mixed Ability Work in Comprehensive Schools*; London: HMSO.

Isherwood, E.B. (1973) 'The principal and his authority'; *High Schools Journal* 56.

Keys, W. and Fernandes, C. (1993) *What do Students Think about School?*; Windsor: NFER.

Kyriacou, C. (1989) 'The nature and prevalence of teacher stress' in Cole, M. and Walker, S. *Teaching and Stress*; Milton Keynes: Open University Press.

La Fontaine, J. (1990) *Bullying: the Child's View*; London: Calouste Gulbenkian Foundation.

Lawrence, J., Steed, D. and Young, P. (1984) *Disruptive Children, Disruptive Schools*; London: Croom Helm.

Little, J.W. (1982) 'Norms of collegiality and experimentation: workplace conditions of school success'; *American Research Journal* 19(3).

Mancini, V., Wuest, D., Vantine, K. and Clark, E. (1984) 'The case for instruction and supervision in interaction analysis on burned out teachers: its effects on teaching behaviours, level of burnout and academic learning time'; *Journal of Teaching in Physical Education* 3(2).

Margerison, C. (1978) *Influencing Organisational Change*; London: Institute of Personnel Management.

Marshall, C. and Mitchell, B. (1989) 'Women's careers as a critique of the administrative culture'; paper presented at the American Research Association annual conference.

Martens, R. (1982) *Sport Competition Anxiety Test*; Champaign, Illinois: Human Kinetics Publishers.

Morgan, C., Hall, V. and Mackay, H. (1983) *The Selection of Secondary Headteachers*; Milton Keynes: Open University Press.

Morgan, C., Hall, V. and Mackay, H. (1984) *A Handbook on Selecting Senior Staff for Schools*; Milton Keynes: Open University Press.

Mortimore, P., Sammons, P., Stoll, L., Lewis, D. and Ecob, R. (1988) *School Matters*; London: Open Books.

NAGM (1988) *Building an Effective School Governing Body*; London: National Association of Governors and Managers.

NASSP (1982) *The Effective Principal*; Renton, Virginia: National Association of Secondary School Principals.

NCC (1990) *The Whole Curriculum*; York: National Curriculum Council.

Novak, J.D. and Gowin, D.B. (1984) *Learning how to Learn*; Cambridge: Cambridge University Press.

Oldroyd, D. and Hall, V. (1988) *Managing Professional Development and INSET*; Bristol: National Development Centre for School Management Training.

Oxley, H. (1987) *The Principles of Public Relations*; London: Kogan Page.

Poster, C. and Poster, D. (1991) *Teacher Appraisal: a guide to training*; London: Routledge.

Reid, K., Hopkins, D. and Holly, P.(1987) *Towards the Effective School*; Oxford: Blackwell.

Reynolds, D. (ed.) (1985) *Studying School Effectiveness*; Sussex: Falmer.

Rolph, S. (1990) *Budgeting and Equipment for Schools*; London: Hobson.

Rutter, M., Maughan, B., Mortimore, P., Ouston, J. and Smith, A. (1979) *Fifteen Thousand Hours*; London: Open Books.

Sallis, J. (1990) 'Working with others' in *Governing Bodies Now: report of DES conference*; November.

SEAC (1990) *Assessing the National Curriculum*; London: Schools Examination and Assessment Council.

Stewart, R. (1967) *The Reality of Management*; London: Pan Piper.

Stillman, A. and Mychell, K. (1984) *School to School: the Isle of Wight study*; Windsor: NFER–Nelson.

Strain, M. (1990) 'Resource management in schools: some conceptual and practical considerations' in Cave, E. and Wilkinson, C. (eds) *Local Management of Schools: some practical issues*; London: Routledge.

Suffolk Education Department (1987) *Teacher Appraisal: a practical guide, part 3*; Ipswich: Suffolk County Council.

Surrey Education Department (1990) *School Development Plans*; Kingston: Surrey County Council.

Swann Report (1981) *Education for All*; London: HMSO.

Taylor, F. (1992) 'The law, the school, the miscreant and his mother' in *TES*, February.

Tizard, B., Blatchford, P., Burke, J., Farquhar, C. and Lewis, I. (1988) *Young Children at School in the Inner City*; Brighton: Lawrence Erlbaum Associates.

West Sussex Education Committee (1991) *Gen: the governors' newsletter*, March; Brighton: West Sussex County Council.

Wheldall, K. and Merrett, F. (1984) *Positive Teaching: the Behavioural Approach*; London: Unwin.

Wilson, A.T.M. (1967) *Human Relations in Management*; Cincinnati, Ohio: South Western Publishing Company.

Woods, P.(1989) 'Stress and the teacher role' in Cole, M. and Walker, S. (eds) *Teaching and Stress*; Milton Keynes: Open University Press.

Wragg, E.C. (1987) *Teacher Appraisal: a practical guide*; London: Macmillan.

Yorke, D.A. and Bakewell, C.J. (1991) 'Choice of secondary school: consumer behaviour and implications for local management of schools'; in *International Journal of Management Education* 1(2).

Index